ENGLISH FOR WORK

EVERYDAY
BUSINESS
ENGLISH

Ian Badger

Longman

Pearson Education Limited
Edinburgh Gate, Harlow,
Essex, CM20 2JE, England
and Associated Companies throughout the world

www.longman.com
Copyright © Ian Badger 2003

All rights reserved; no part of this publication may be reproduced, stored in a retrieval system, or transmitted in any form or by any means, electronic, mechanical, photocopying, recording, or otherwise without the prior written permission of the Publishers. The moral right of the author has been asserted.

First published 2003
Third impression 2004
ISBN 0 582 53957 9

Set in Univers Condensed 10pt
Printed in Great Britain by Scotprint, Haddington

Designed and typeset by Rock Graphics

Illustrations by Anthony Seldon

Acknowledgements
I would especially like to thank Helen Parker for her support in developing this series, Julie Nowell, Judith Greet, Teresa Miller, Elaine Murray, Maria Keller and Fiona Walker for their valuable comments and assistance throughout the writing process, Diane Winkleby for her help with the British/American differences boxes and the many students from UPM-Kymmene, Metso Paper, Goldwell Gmbh and BMES for their help in piloting the materials.

Cover photograph copyright © Photonica/Jed Share

Contents

Introduction   page 5

1 Telephoning
page 7

Dialogues 1
- Beginning a call
- Checking information
- Asking the caller to hold
- Asking a caller to leave a message
- Making sure you understand
- Ending a call
- An automated message

Dialogues 2
- A voicemail message
- Leaving a message
- You can't talk
- The reason for calling
- You can't hear the caller
- You have to end the call

2 A company visit
page 15

Dialogues 1
- Directions to the office
- Getting lost
- Arrival
- Meeting

Dialogues 2
- Introducing a company (1)
- Introducing a company (2)
- Company history
- A tour of the office

Dialogues 3
- Business activities (1)
- Business activities (2)
- Markets
- The competition

3 Job information
page 25

Dialogues 1
- Responsibilities
- Qualifications for the job
- A typical day
- Discussing a new appointment

Dialogues 2
- Working conditions
- Financial rewards
- Job benefits
- Redundancy and retirement

4 Presentations
page 33

Dialogues 1
- Setting the scene
- Moving on
- Dealing with questions
- Dealing with the unexpected
- Recapping
- Coming to an end

Dialogues 2
- Some facts and figures
- Predictions
- Trends (upwards)
- Trends (downwards)
- Trends (steady)

5 Meetings
page 41

Dialogues 1
- Setting up a meeting (by phone)
- Postponing a meeting (by phone)
- Setting up a meeting (a voicemail message)
- Confirming a meeting by email

Dialogues 2
- Working through an agenda
- Reporting back to a meeting
- Reaching an agreement
- Making a point

Dialogues 3
- A follow-up phone call (1)
- A follow-up phone call (2)
- Action points (on a dictaphone)
- Sending minutes by email

6 Entertaining and socialising
page 51

Dialogues 1
- Coffee or tea?
- Translating the menu
- Ordering a meal (1)
- Ordering a meal (2)
- Paying the bill

Dialogues 2
- Where you live
- Starting a conversation
- Family matters
- Cultural advice
- Sensitive issues

7 Travel
page 59

Dialogues 1
- Checking in for a flight
- Hiring a car
- Taking the train
- Booking a hotel
- Checking into a hotel

Dialogues 2
- At the check-in desk
- A flight delay
- A tight connection
- A hotel mix-up
- A payment problem

8 Emailing
page 67

Messages 1
- A first contact
- A formal message
- Everyday matters
- A future meeting
- Declining an invitation

Messages 2
- Saying thank you (1)
- Saying thank you (2)
- An invitation
- Accepting an invitation
- Passing on good wishes

Messages 3
- Problems
- Good news
- A general announcement
- For information

Glossary   page 79

Answers   page 88

Introduction

English for Work
The books in this series present and practise spoken English and practical writing for everyday communication; they feature key words and expressions which will help you in a wide range of work situations. The target language is introduced through short dialogues and texts, and developed in language notes and practice exercises.

The dialogues are recorded on an accompanying CD. The accents featured are predominantly British English, but comments on American usage are included in the notes.

At the back of each book there is a glossary which contains highlighted language from the dialogues. Translations of the glossary, in selected languages, can be downloaded from the Longman website, **www.longman-elt.com**.

The series is intended for pre-intermediate/intermediate level learners.

Everyday Business English
Everyday Business English is suitable for anyone who needs to work in the business world, and for students in adult education classes, schools, colleges and universities.

The book contains a range of language common to all who need to use English in their business lives. Whether you use English in meetings, presentations, on the phone or in emails, you will find language to help you work more effectively in this book.

Some of the everyday business English themes included in *Everyday Business English* are covered in greater depth in the other titles in the series:

Business Presentations
Everyday Technical English
Everyday Business Writing

How to use the book
You can work through *Everyday Business English* from start to finish or choose a chapter depending on your business need.

Start a chapter by listening to and repeating the *Useful phrases*. Then listen to the dialogues and study the accompanying notes. Certain phrases have been highlighted that have particular language features associated with them. However, it is worthwhile noting other phrases that appear in the dialogues, which are equally important and can also be seen as key phrases. Use a dictionary to check your understanding of the language presented.

On the notes pages you will find boxes containing notes on some differences between everyday British and American usage.

After studying the dialogues and notes, work through the exercises. You can refer back to the dialogues and notes as necessary. Answers and possible responses to the more 'open-ended' exercises are given at the end of the book.

Finally, refer to the glossary at the back of the book and test yourself on your understanding of key expressions. Write translations of these expressions, again using a dictionary if necessary. Visit the *English for Work* page on the Longman website where you will find translations of the key phrases in a number of languages.

You can use this book for self study or with a teacher. Good luck and enjoy building your 'everyday business English' skills!

Ian Badger, Bristol 2003

Some recommended materials to accompany the *English for Work* series:
Longman Business English Dictionary
Penguin Quick Guides: Business English Phrases
Penguin Quick Guides: Business English Verbs
Penguin Quick Guides: Business English Words
Penguin Quick Guides: Computer English

1 Telephoning

**Some useful phrases.
Listen to the recording and repeat.**

Can I speak to Peter Safin, please?
Speaking.
Are you busy?
Can I call you back?

Please hold on.
Sorry to keep you waiting.
I'll transfer you.

What's the area code for Dublin?
Dial 9 to get an outside line.
Press the star key twice.

This is a very bad line.
You're breaking up.
The reception is very bad.

Would you like to leave a message?
Leave a message on my voicemail.
I'm in a meeting. I'll call you back.

I think we've covered everything.
Speak to you soon.
Bye for now.

SORRY TO KEEP YOU WAITING SO LONG. ARE YOU STILL THERE?

Dialogues 1

Beginning a call

- **A**: I'd like to speak to Max Reed, please.
- **B**: Just one moment. I'll connect you … You're through now.
- **C**: Max Reed speaking.
- **A**: Hi, Max. Simon here.
- **C**: Hi, Simon. How are you?
- **A**: Fine. And you?

Checking information

- **A**: Hello.
- **B**: Hello, John. Sven here. Did you get my email?
- **A**: Yes, it's right here in front of me.
- **B**: Fine. I thought it would be quicker to phone than send you another message. I wanted to run through some of the arrangements for Tuesday…

Asking the caller to hold

- **A**: Sorry to keep you waiting so long. Could you hold on a little longer? The network is very slow today.
- **B**: How long do you think it is going to take to find the information?
- **A**: It won't be long now. Right. Here we are. The figures you need are …

Asking the caller to leave a message

- **A**: I'm trying to get hold of someone in your sales department. Are you having problems with your phone system? I was cut off earlier and now there is no reply.
- **B**: Just a moment, please. I'll try the number for you. Yes, I'm afraid there's no reply from the department. They must be at lunch. Would you like to leave a message and I'll get someone to call you when they get back.
- **A**: Thanks. My name's Baz Mechot and the number is 453980.

Making sure you understand

- **A**: Can I speak to Teresa Riller? I understand that she is looking after Sales while Marco Stam is on parental leave.
- **B**: That's right, but I'm afraid she's not here at the moment. Can I take a message?
- **A**: Thanks. Could you say that Pieter Baumgartner called and ask her to call me back?
- **B**: Can you spell your name, please?
- **A**: Baumgartner is B-a-u-m-g-a-r-t-n-e-r. I'm at the Rainbow Hotel in room 13.
- **B**: Is that 13, one three, or 30, three zero?
- **A**: Thirteen, one three.
- **B**: Thanks. I'll pass on the message.

Ending a call

- **A**: … OK. Have we covered everything?
- **B**: I think so. You just need to let me know when you can send the report.
- **A**: That's right. I'll send you a message when I get back to the office. Anyway, thanks for calling.
- **B**: No problem. I'll wait to hear from you.

Notes

I'd like to speak to Max Reed, please.
Some other phrases for checking if someone is available:
Is Max Reed there?
Can I talk to Max Reed?
Is Max Reed available?

Hi, Max. Simon here.
This is an informal greeting. More formal greetings include:
Hello, Mr Reed. This is Simon Speedwell speaking.
Mr Reed. Hello, it's Simon Speedwell here.

I wanted to run through …
We often introduce the topic politely by using the past tense. We can also use *I'd like to…*
For example:
I wanted to run through the arrangements.
I wanted to ask you a question.
I wanted to know about your travel plans.
I'd like to ask you a question.

Sorry to keep you waiting …
Some other phrases to use when someone is waiting on the phone:
Could you hold on?
Do you mind holding.

Would you like to leave a message?
Would is used to introduce a polite offer. Note also:
Would you like me to check?
Would you like to call back later?
Would you like to hold on?

… I'll get someone to call you when they get back.
Note the use of the simple present tense *when they get …* in this sentence:
*I'll call you **if I can**.*
*I'll phone you **when they arrive**.*
*I'll let you know **if I hear anything**.*
*I'll fax you **if I remember the name**.*

I understand that she is looking after Sales …
Language that indicates that you already have some information:
I understand that you're coming to Warsaw next week.
I hear that Pedro is moving to Singapore.
I see (that) they're going to open a new office in Paris.

… Marco Stam is on parental leave.
Some other reasons for absence include:
He's on paternity leave.
She's on maternity leave.
She's taking compassionate leave.
He's ill.
She's on holiday.
He's left for the day.

… I'm afraid she's not here at the moment.
Use *I'm afraid* or *I'm Sorry to* when passing on unwelcome information.
I'm afraid I can't help you.
I'm sorry I'm going to be late.
I'm afraid I can't find the information you need.

Have we covered everything?
Note how we signal that a call is coming to an end:
So is that everything?
Is that all?

Anyway, thanks for calling.
Other ways of bringing a call to an end:
Right, I'll check the details and call you back.
I think that's everything.
Is there anything else?

British/American differences
Some differences between British and American English:

British	American
parental leave	family leave
compassionate leave	In American English the term *bereavement leave* is also used.
She's on holiday.	She's on vacation.

Dialogues 2

A voicemail message

'This is Ann Forsell's voicemail. I'm sorry I can't take your call at the moment, but please leave a message and I'll get back to you. Alternatively you can leave a message with my assistant. His number is 0046, (that's the country code for Sweden), 01, (that's the area code), 2132. Many thanks.'

Leaving a message

'Hi, Fiona. I've been trying to get hold of you all morning so I hope you get this. Please call Sara Remondi as soon as you can. It's about the meeting next month. Unfortunately I can't make it so we need to talk urgently. It's two o'clock my time by the way and I'll be going home in three hours. Bye for now.'

You can't talk

- A: Hello.
- B: Hi, John. Can you talk?
- A: Not really. I'm in a meeting. Can I call you back in, say, fifteen minutes?
- B: Sure. Speak to you later. It isn't urgent.

The reason for calling

- A: Can you hear me now? I couldn't hear you very well earlier. The reception was terrible. Anyway, how are you?
- B: Fine. I was just ringing to check the time for next week's meeting. Is it still three o'clock?

You can't hear the caller

- A: Hello.
- B: Hello. Sorry, I can't hear you very well. I'm in a restaurant and they have just started playing some loud music.
- A: I didn't catch that.
- B: I'll just go outside. Just a moment. Can you hear me now?
- A: Yes, that's much better. I'm glad you're enjoying yourself.

You have to end the call

- A: John, Peter has just arrived. I'll call you when I get back to London.
- B: Fine. I'll be here until 5. Speak to you later. Bye.
- A: Bye.

An automated message

'Welcome to Haznor Business Systems. This is a toll-free number. Please choose one of the following four options. If you are calling about an existing order, please press 1. If you wish to place a new order, press 2...'

Notes

This is Ann Forsell's voicemail.
Some other formal opening phrases for voicemail are:
You're through to Ann Forsell's voicemail.
You've reached Ann's voicemail.
An informal opening:
Hi. Ann here. Sorry I can't take your call at the moment but leave a message and I'll get back to you.

It's about the meeting next month.
Calls often begin with:
I'm calling/ringing about (your flight).
John, about (your flight to Paris).

... I can't make it ...
Make is often used instead of *attend* in informal usage:
Unfortunately, I can't make the next meeting.
I can't make Friday but Thursday would be fine.
Will you be able to make it?

Can you talk?
Other useful phrases for checking if the person you want to talk to is free, and some replies:
Are you busy?
Are you free to talk?
Have you got two minutes?

Can I call you back?
It's difficult at the moment.
This is a good time to talk.

I'm in a meeting.
Some other reasons why you cannot take a call:
I'm not at my desk.
I'm driving. (I'll just pull over.)
I'm just getting on a train.
I've just arrived at the airport.
I haven't got my diary with me.

I was just ringing to check the time ...
I was just ringing/calling ... is a useful alternative way to start a call:
I was just calling about the meeting next Friday.
I was just ringing to see if everything's OK for tomorrow.
I was just calling to ask for some advice.

Sorry, I can't hear you very well.
Some other phrases to use when reception is bad:
Sorry, could you repeat that?
Could you say that again?
I'm sorry, I didn't catch that.
I'm afraid the line's bad. Did you say fifteen?
Could you speak louder? The line's very bad.

I'll just go outside.
Use *will* when you offer or promise to do something.
I'll call you when I get back to London.
I'll be here until 5.
I'll tell her you called.
I'll make sure she gets the message.
I'll get back to you as soon as I can.

If you are calling about an existing order, please press 1.
Some other 'automated' instructions:
Press the star key twice.
Press the hash/square key.
Press 5 to speak to the operator.
Please replace the handset.

British/American differences

British	American
Differences in expressing time:	
Monday to Friday	Monday through Friday
ten past six	ten after six
the ninth of December	December ninth
24-hour clock:	12-hour clock:
9:00, 17:00	9 a.m., 5 p.m.

Note: In the UK both 12-hour and 24-hour clocks are used but in the US the 24-hour clock is generally used only by the military.

Some differences in saying telephone numbers:

360-4458 = three six oh, double-four five eight	360-4458 = three six zero, forty-four fifty-eight

Other differences

Mobile phone (p12)	cell(ular) phone
directory enquiries (p13)	directory assistance/ information
dialled (p14)	dialed

Practice

1 Complete the sentences using the verbs from the box below. Use each verb once only.

| press | try | call | hear | leave | keep | want | ~~say~~ | hold | hang | get |

EXAMPLE: I'm trying to ...**get**... hold of Peter Ince.

a Would you like to .... a message?

b I can't .... you very well. Please speak up.

c Could you .... on, please? I won't be long.

d Sorry to .... you waiting.

e Can I .... you later?

f If you .... to place an order, ... the star key.

g I'll .... someone to call you later.

h He didn't .... when he would be back in the office.

i Please don't .... up. I'll .... the number again.

2 Write what you would say in these situations. Refer to the dialogues and notes.

EXAMPLE: You are the manager. The phone rings and you pick it up. The caller asks 'Is that the manager?' What do you say?

.....**Yes, [Tina Forget] speaking.**.....................................

a Your female colleague is off work as she has just had a baby. What do you say to the caller who wants to speak to her?

   ....

b You are in a meeting and you receive a call on your mobile phone. You cannot speak. What do you say?

   ....

c Leave a message on your colleague Peter's voicemail. Say that you called and ask him to call back when he gets the message.

   ....

d You don't catch the caller's name. Ask him to spell it.

   ....

e A colleague phones to let you know her hotel room number but you can't hear her very well. You are not sure whether it is fifteen or fifty. What do you say?

   ....

3 Complete the sentences with a preposition.

EXAMPLE: I'll call you ...in...... ten minutes.

a I'm trying to connect you. Could you hold ....?
b When are you going .... holiday?
c I'm calling .... the order I placed last week.
d Could you pass .... a message for me?
e I'll write to you .... two weeks' time.
f Tom is .... paternity leave.

4 Choose an appropriate response.

1	What's the time in New York?	a	Sure, what's your number?
2	When will Eleanor be back?	b	Speaking.
3	Is that Tariq Meltam?	c	Yes, of course. Let me just find a pen.
4	Is Mr Rotund there?	d	Nine a.m.
5	Have a good weekend.	e	Yes, it's right here.
6	Did you get my email?	f	Yes, it's 09.
7	Could you call me back?	g	Yes, he has just come into the office.
8	Can you take a message for me?	h	In ten days' time.
9	Do you know the code for Helsinki?	i	Thanks. You too.

5 Complete the sentences with *will* or the present simple tense.

EXAMPLE: I (give) him the message when I (see) him.

   I'll give him the message when I see him. ....

a I (tell) him you called.

   ....

b If I (find) the information, I (let) you know immediately.

   ....

c If Peter (not come back) from sick leave soon, we (need) to find a replacement.

   ....

d If you (push) that button, you (disconnect) the caller.

   ....

e What (do) if you (not find) Sergei's number?

   ....

f If I (not find) his number, I (call) directory enquiries.

   ....

6 Complete the sentences with one of the alternatives.

EXAMPLE: Press the ..hash..... key.   hash/button/door

a   Replace the ....   reception/handset/operator

b   Make a .... call.   toll-free/star/line

c   .... Anne's voice mail.   Here is/This is/Hello to

d   I couldn't .... hold of John.   get/take/make

e   Please don't .... up.   hang/hold/take

f   Don't forget to .... your mobile phone.   turn off/close/drop

g   Did you dial the .... code first?   area/secret/town

7 Put the dialogue in the right order

a   Speaking.
b   Hi Tarmo.
c   Thanks, Tarmo
d   I'll do it now.
e   Of course,
f   Did you get my message?
g   You'd like me to send directions to the office.
h   Can I speak to Tarmo Star please?
i   Yes that's right.
j   Could you send them today?
k   Yes I did.
l   See you soon.

..h, a,...

8 Match the two parts of the sentences.

1   Press the star key   a   on hold for a minute.
2   Could you leave a message   b   a conference call for next week.
3   I'll call you   c   take the call at the moment.
4   Please wait. I'll just put you d   the wrong number.
5   I'm sorry, I must have dialled e   to return to the main menu.
6   We need to set up   f   with directory enquiries.
7   I need to check the number   g   for me on my voicemail?
8   I'm sorry but I can't   h   when I get back to my office.

2 A company visit

**Some useful phrases.
Listen to the recording and repeat.**

Could you give me directions to your office?
Just follow the signs.
Go past the station and take the first turning on the left.
You'll see the office on the right-hand side.
I've left my car in a reserved space

I have an appointment with Hans Ekburg.
Take the lift to the fourth floor.
His office is the fifth on the right, along the corridor.
Hello Hans, I'd like you to meet our Marketing Manager.
Pleased to meet you.

Tell me something about the company.
What does the company do?
We're in the transport business.
We employ just under 5 000 people worldwide.

The company was set up five years ago.
We're the largest manufacturer in the country.
North America is our biggest market in terms of sales by region.
We have an excellent reputation for service.
Business is booming.

Dialogues 1

Directions to the office

A: Hi, Rosa. It's June here. I'm in the town centre outside the bus station. **Could you tell me how to get to your office from here?**

B: Sure. Follow the signs for Frankfurt. **After about two kilometres, you'll see a garage on your right.** Carry on for another 200 metres and then turn left. Our office is on the left-hand side, just before a railway bridge. When you arrive, **park in one of the visitors' spaces** just outside the main building.

A: Thanks, Rosa. See you soon.

Getting lost

A: Hi, Carla.

B: Hello, Bob. Is everything all right?

A: Not really. I'm lost. **I'm calling from a service station** on the E7 just south of a place called Melton. I don't have a map with me so could you direct me to the factory.

B: Sure. **Take the first left after the service station** and follow the road to Porlock. Pass the shopping centre on your right and then take the first left. **Carry on for three kilometres** and you'll see the factory.

A: Thanks.

Arrival

A: Good morning, can I help you?

B: Yes, **I have an appointment with Hans Ekburg.** Could you tell him I'm here? I've left my car in a reserved space.

A: That's OK, I'll take the car registration number. Could you write your name here please and wear this? [*hands over a visitor's badge*]. **Do you know the building?**

B: I'm afraid I don't.

A: OK, go up these stairs and take the lift to the third floor. **Mr Ekburg's office is the fifth on the right, along the corridor.**

B: Thanks.

Meeting

A: **Hello, John. Good to see you again.**

B: And you.

A: John, **I'd like you to meet Lera Berman,** our Marketing Manager.

C: Hello, John. Pleased to meet you. **Did you have a good journey?**

B: Yes, very good. The directions were very clear.

Notes

Could you tell me how to get to the office from here?
We also say:
Can you tell me the way to …?
How do I get to …?
Excuse me, where is the main office?

After about two kilometres you'll see a garage on your right.
Some other landmarks:
You'll pass some shops.
Then you'll see a large red building in front of you.
Keep going and you'll come to the entrance gate.

Park in one of the visitors' spaces …
Parking the car:
I've left my car in a reserved space.
There are some spaces reserved for visitors.
Can I park here?
Is this space reserved?

I'm calling from a service station …
When you need to say where you are:
I'm calling from the train.
I'm on the M1 motorway.
I'm calling from a service station on the M4.

Take the first left after the service station …
Some useful directions when you are driving:
Carry on for three kilometres.
Take the second exit at the roundabout.
Turn left at the junction.
Go straight across the crossroads.
At the traffic lights, turn right.

Carry on for three kilometres …
Other expressions for talking about distance:
Carry/Drive on for another ten kilometres.
… until you come to a service station.
It's two hundred metres past the service station on the right-hand side.

I have an appointment with Hans Ekburg.
Note the statements and responses:
I'm here to see Hans Ekburg.
Can I have your name, please?
Could you sign in please?
Is Hans Ekburg in/available?
Yes, he's expecting you.

Do you know the building?
Checking if a visitor knows his/her way around a building:
Have you been here before?
When were you last here?
I haven't been here before.

Mr Ekburg's office is the fifth on the right, along the corridor.
Some other office locations:
It's opposite the lift.
It's just past the coffee machine.
Go through the automatic doors.

Hello, John. Good to see you again.
An informal greeting. Other possibilities:
Hi, John. How are you?
How's life?
How's it going?
Possible responses:
Fine thanks.
I'm very well.

I'd like you to meet Lera Berman, …
Some language of introductions:
I'd like to introduce Lera Berman.
Have you (already) met?
Yes, we met last year.

Did you have a good journey?
We can also say:
How was the journey?
How was the flight/traffic?

British/American differences

British	American
service station	gas or filling station
shopping centre	(shopping) mall
car registration number	license plate number
lift	elevator
shops	stores
motorway	freeway/expressway/Interstate
roundabout	traffic circle
crossroads	intersection
traffic lights	stop lights

Dialogues 2

Introducing a company (1)

A: **We're in the label business.** We produce all kinds of labels – price labels, bottle labels, even postage stamps. We have factories in France, Germany, Malaysia, China and the UK.
B: How many people work for the company?
A: **We employ just over 5 000 people worldwide.** There are around 400 employees in this factory.
B: Is business going well?
A: Yes it is, and **it's growing all the time.**

Introducing a company (2)

A: So, **tell me more about your mailing business.**
B: Sure. We provide a complete packaging and mailing service for our customers. We now have branches all over the south of the country and we have plans to open new branches in the north.
A: What kind of company are you?
B: **We're a private limited company.** We're not listed on **the Stock Exchange** … yet.

Company history

A: So, **how long have you been on this site?**
B: We moved here five years ago. Before that, we were in a very small office building in the centre of town.
A: And **when was the company set up?**
B: Ten years ago – by Simon Donna who is still the Managing Director. He started the company with just two employees.
A: That's very impressive.

A tour of the office

A: **Let me show you round the office.** Our sales representatives work in this **open plan area**. The room in the corner is Brit Gamlin's office. She's the Senior Sales Manager here. Do you know her?
B: No, I don't. Has she been here long?
A: No, she joined the company two months ago. Come with me, **I'll introduce you to her.**
A: Hello, Brit. I'd like you to meet Olivier Blaireau from the Paris office.
C: Pleased to meet you Olivier. How are things in Paris?

Notes

We're in the label business.
Some other businesses:
the transport business/the paper business
the I.T. industry/the steel industry
the retail trade/the fashion trade

We employ just over 5 000 people worldwide.
Other ways to talk about employee numbers:
We have just under 5 000 employees.
We have 5 000 people working for us.
5 000 people work for us.

... it's growing all the time.
Describing how a business is going:
The company is doing well/badly.
Things are going well/badly.
Profits are up/down.

... tell me more about your mailing business.
Other useful opening remarks:
What does the company do?
What business are you in?
I hear you work for a mailing business.

We're a private limited company.
Compare with a *public limited company* (plc). The public can buy shares in a public limited company but not in a private limited company.

Some other types of business:
a sole trader (where one person owns the business)
a partnership (a business owned by two or more people)
a family business

... the Stock Exchange ...
The market where stocks and shares are bought and sold.

... how long have you been on this site?
We can also talk about premises (land and buildings) and location (place):
Our current premises are very convenient.
I preferred our previous location in the centre of town.

... when was the company set up?
Other ways to talk about the start of a company:
When was it established?
When was it founded?
It was founded by General Kilbride in 1922.

Let me show you around the office.
Language for 'guiding' people round the office:
Come with me.
Come this way.
Over there you can see the Manager's office.
This is where we handle orders.

... open plan area.
An office area where staff members work in one large, often partitioned, space – not in separate offices. Also known as an *open plan office*.

... I'll introduce you to her.
We can also say:
I'd like to introduce you to Brit Gamlin.
You must meet Brit Gamlin.
Let me introduce you.

British/American differences

British	American
private limited company	company or corporation
limited (Ltd)	incorporated (Inc.)
the retail trade	retail business
public limited company (plc)	a publicly-traded company
a sole trader	a sole proprietor

Dialogues 3

Business activities (1)

A: We're the second largest manufacturer in the country of glass for the car industry. One in three cars in this country uses our glass.

B: How many plants do you have?

A: We have five domestic plants but we also have factories in ten other countries. As well as supplying the car industry, we sell glass for buses, trains, ships and aircraft.

Business activities (2)

A: Tell me more about the company.

B: Basically we run a so-called 'shopping search' website. If you visit our site, you can find links to a wide range of products and services. You can compare prices from various shops and find the best deal.

A: That sounds very interesting, but is it secure?

B: Yes, in my view it's far more secure than buying over the phone.

Markets

A: Where are your biggest markets?

B: In terms of sales by region, Europe is by far the biggest market with 60 per cent of our total sales. North America accounts for 15 per cent, Asia-Pacific is 10 per cent – the Chinese market is particularly strong, South America is 8 per cent and the rest of the world is 7 per cent.

A: I think you'd better write that down for me! Why are things going so well in China?

B: The Chinese economy is booming and we have a very good sales force there.

The competition

A: Who are your main competitors?

B: It depends on the region. There are a lot of local producers in Europe and we cannot compete with them on price. However, our reputation for service is excellent. We are well known in the market for high quality and reliability.

A: What about the Japanese market?

B: We cannot compete in Japan. High transport costs make it very unprofitable to do business. Maybe things will change in the future.

Notes

We're the second largest manufacturer in the country ...
Talking about the size of the company:
We're by far the largest producers of ...
We're the third biggest in the country.
We're among the largest/smallest in the region.

As well as supplying the car industry, we sell ...
Use as well as for emphasis. We can also say:
In addition to supplying the car industry, we supply many other customers.

... we run a so-called 'shopping search' website.
The speaker could also say:
It's what we call a 'shopping search' website.
These phrases show that the words *shopping search* are known to people 'in the business' but not to others.

You can compare prices from various shops ...
We can also say:
You can make comparisons between shops.
You can compare A with B.

... in my view it's far more secure ...
If you are not so sure of your facts, you might say:
As far as I know, it's more secure.

In terms of sales by region, ...
in terms (of) is a useful phrase:
What does that mean in terms of employment?
In terms of profitability, it means that ...
Can you give us the figures in percentage terms?

North America accounts for 15 per cent, ...
This means that sales to North America represent/are fifteen per cent of sales.
Note that we say 'fifteen <u>per</u> cent'
(**NOT** pro cent).

The Chinese economy is booming ...
Some terms to describe the state of a market:
Demand is strong.
Demand is very weak.
There is a steady demand in Australia.
The market for our products is growing/falling.

... we cannot compete with them on price.
Ways of talking about competition:
But we can compete with them in terms of service/speed of delivery.
Our prices are very competitive.
We've become very uncompetitive in that market.

We are well known in the market ...
Ways of describing reputation:
We have a good reputation.
We have an excellent name.
Everyone knows us.
We are well established in the market.

... transport costs make it very unprofitable ...
Talking about profit and loss:
It's a very profitable business.
We're not making much profit.
We're making a loss.
We're finally making a profit.

British/American differences	
British	**American**
transport costs	transportation costs
We're making a loss.	We're operating at a loss./We're taking a loss.

Practice

1 Complete the sentences with a preposition.

EXAMPLE: You need to take the lift ...**to**...... the third floor.

a Take the third turning .... the left.
b Park .... one of the visitors' spaces.
c We are .... far the largest manufacturer.
d One .... three of our plants is making a loss.
e There is no profit .... it.
f Tell me about your sales .... region.
g We are very competitive .... terms of price.
h Are you listed .... the Stock Exchange?
i What kind of business are you .... ?

2 Complete the sentences using the words in the box below. Use each word once only.

| reputation | demand | corridor | profit | site |
| partnership | registration | ~~map~~ | lift | |

EXAMPLE: Could you give me directions? I don't have a ..**map**......

a Do you need my car .... number?
b How long have you had offices on this .... ?
c You can use the stairs, but it's quicker to take the ....
d My office is along the .... on the right.
e After two years of making losses, we are now making a ....
f There is a growing .... for our products in the Middle East.
g My brother and I went into .... three years ago.
h We have an excellent .... for quality.

3 Choose an appropriate response.

1 Did you have a good journey?   a No, it's a partnership.
2 Is it a limited company?   b Just over five years ago.
3 When was the company set up?   c Yes, that's right.
4 Have you been on this site long?   d Thanks, I can manage.
5 I hear you're in the transport business? e Yes, very good thanks.
6 What kind of company is it?   f Yes, we met last year.
7 Can I help?   g It's a small family business.
8 Do you know Gunilla?   h Yes, for twenty years.

4 Write what you would say.

a Direct someone to the factory.

....
....
....
....
....
....

b Direct someone to your office.

....
....
....
....
....
....

c Explain where you parked your car.

....
....
....
....
....
....
....

d Explain where you are.

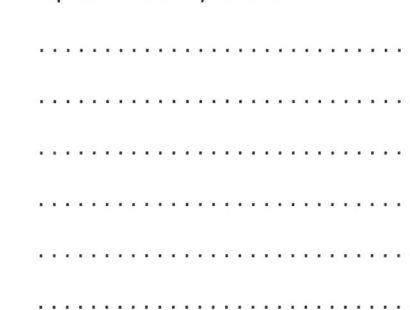

....
....
....
....
....
....
....

5 Write down a question for the following answers. Refer to the dialogues and notes.

EXAMPLE: What kind of business are you in?
We're in the shipping business.

a How many ....?
We employ just over 200 people.

b Are ....?
No, we're not a partnership – we're a limited company.

c How long ....?
We have been on this site for three years.

d Do ....?
Yes, I do. The working atmosphere is very good now.

e Where ....?
In terms of region, the biggest market is North America.

f Who ....?
I suppose our biggest competitors are companies in Thailand and Indonesia.

g Can you tell me ....?
Follow the road to Trieste and you'll see the factory on the right.

6 Rewrite the following in another way. Refer to the dialogues and notes.

EXAMPLE: I have an appointment with Jan Pickero.
I'm here to see Jan Pickero.

a I've parked in a reserved space.

b Could you tell me the way to the main office?

c I'd like to you to meet our marketing manager.

d How was the journey?

e When was the company established?

f We are one of the largest manufacturers in the region.

g We have an excellent name in the market.

3 Job information

**Some useful phrases.
Listen to the recording and repeat.**

I work for a software company.
I'm responsible for the development of new products.
It's a very challenging job.
I report directly to the Managing Director.

The job involves a lot of travelling.
I usually start work at 8 o'clock in the morning.
Do you usually drive to work?

How's the new job?
I really enjoy it.
The salary is good.
I'm very pleased I moved here.

How has the takeover affected you?
Some people are going to lose their jobs.
Some will take early retirement.
There won't be any compulsory redundancies.

We need to recruit a new training manager.
What kind of person are you looking for?
We need someone with excellent communication skills.

I REALLY ENJOY THIS JOB. IT'S A GREAT COMPANY TO WORK FOR.

Dialogues 1

Responsibilities

A: So, what exactly do you do in the company?
B: I'm responsible for new product development. I report directly to the CEO.
A: What does that involve?
B: I supervise a team of designers. We all have to think of new ideas, test them and develop the ones that we think will succeed.
A: It sounds challenging.
B: It is, but I really enjoy it.

Qualifications for the job

A: I hear you studied in Finland.
B: That's right. I did a degree in Engineering at Tampere Technical University and then I worked in a small software company in Helsinki.
A: Why did you decide to stay in Finland?
B: I was very interested in the job. I wanted to put my training into practice. The experience was very good and certainly helped me to get this job.

A typical day

A: What time do you start in the mornings?
B: I aim to get to work by 8 a.m. That means leaving home at 7:30. I usually cycle to work.
A: Are the hours flexible?
B: In theory, yes, but I normally finish at 4 p.m. I sometimes finish earlier if I take a very short lunch break.
A: Do you go out for lunch?
B: Occasionally, but I like eating in the company canteen.

Discussing a new appointment

A: What kind of person are we looking for?
B: We want someone who is already working as a Project Manager in a software house. He or she should have at least three years' experience.
A: What sorts of skills are needed?
B: Excellent communication skills are essential. The person we appoint will have a lot of direct contact with clients – we need someone who can present the company clearly.
A: Absolutely. So where can we find this person?
B: I think we should advertise with an on-line recruitment agency but we may have to use a firm of head-hunters.

Notes

I'm responsible for new product development.
We can also say:
I'm in charge of new product development.
New product development is my responsibility.

I report directly to the CEO.
This means the CEO is my boss.
CEO = Chief Executive Officer
CFO = Chief Financial Officer
MD = Managing Director

What does that involve?
Notice that we use the *-ing* form of the verb after *involve*:
It involves attending a lot of meetings.
It involves working long hours.

It sounds challenging.
challenging means demanding, tough.
The job is a challenge.
I enjoy challenges.

I hear you studied in Finland.
Note how *hear, understand,* and *believe* are used in conversation:
I understand you spent some time in Japan.
I believe you know Don quite well.

Possible responses:
That's right/Not really.
Yes, I was there for two years.
Yes, we're very good friends.

I did a degree in Engineering …
Other language for describing studies:
I did a B.A. (Bachelor of Arts)
I studied for an MSc. (Master of Science)
I completed my studies last year.
I graduated from Oxford University in 1999.

I was very interested in the job.
Note the prepositions:
to be interested <u>in</u>, keen <u>on</u>, fascinated <u>by</u>

I usually cycle to work.
Other ways of getting to work – note the correct prepositions:
I walk/go <u>on</u> foot.
I drive/go <u>by</u> car.
I take the train/go <u>by</u> train.

Are the hours flexible?
Phrases to talk about flexible working:
I work flexible hours.
We have a 'flexitime' system.

… I like eating in the company canteen.
Another person may prefer to have a *takeaway* or to eat:
in a local restaurant.
at his/her desk.
in a sandwich bar.
from a market stall.

Excellent communication skills are essential.
Some key qualifications for a job:
We need someone who is very reliable.
We're looking for someone with strong leadership skills.
We want someone with a good 'track record'.

Absolutely.
In speech, *Absolutely* means I agree/You're right.

… we should advertise with an on-line recruitment agency …
We can find staff in a *recruitment* or *employment agency*.
How do you recruit staff?
Do you advertise in the local/national newspapers?

British/American differences

British	American
flexitime	flextime
takeaway	takeout

Note: *To be keen on* is only used in British English. It is not used at all in American English.

Dialogues 2

Working conditions

- **A:** Are you pleased you moved to the Bangkok office?
- **B:** Yes I am. The atmosphere is very relaxed and I have a good group of colleagues. There's a great mix of nationalities and we often go out for dinner or for a drink after work. Everyone is on first name terms.
- **A:** Don't you find it very hot there?
- **B:** Bangkok is hot, yes, but the offices are very comfortable. All the buildings and cars are air-conditioned. I have no regrets about moving.

Financial rewards

- **A:** What kind of salary do you think we should offer for the new sales manager's job in Almaty?
- **B:** It's difficult to say. We would normally pay $50 000 a year plus commission for a job with these responsibilities, but I don't know about the cost of living in Kazakhstan and I have no idea about the level of local salaries.
- **A:** Neither have I. I'll talk to Balgira Karakas about it. She's originally from Almaty – I think she's working in our Dacca office at the moment.

Job benefits

- **A:** How's the new job?
- **B:** I'm very happy with it. The salary is reasonable – not quite as good as in the last job but the company really looks after its people.
- **A:** How do you mean?
- **B:** Well, I have free use of the company gym and health club, they pay for all my phone calls and I get excellent medical insurance. Sickness pay and holidays are very good and the promotion prospects are excellent.
- **A:** You're lucky.
- **B:** Yes, I am – they even give us a season ticket for the local football team!

Retirement and redundancy

- **A:** How has the takeover affected the company?
- **B:** Well, the new owners are going to close down a plant in Manila and another in Dubai. About 300 people are going to lose their jobs.
- **A:** That's terrible.
- **B:** Actually it's not quite as bad as it seems. Most of the staff will be offered jobs in other plants and quite a few want to take early retirement.
- **A:** So there are no compulsory redundancies?
- **B:** Very few.
- **A:** That's good news.

Notes

The atmosphere is very relaxed ...
>The working atmosphere can be *formal* or *informal*. It can also be *stressful* or *relaxed*.

Everyone is on first name terms.
>In an informal environment, staff are probably *on first name terms* – they use first names rather than surnames.

Don't you find it very hot there?
>Note that the use of *Don't* at the beginning of this question expects the answer *Yes*. If the answer is *No*, the speaker must emphasise the answer, e.g.: *Not really. No, not at all.*

I have no regrets about moving.
>Expressing feelings:
>*I don't regret moving here at all.*
>*I'm happy to be here.*
>*I'm very pleased I moved.*

... $50 000 a year plus commission ...
>*Commission* is the payment made to sales people depending on how much they sell.

... the cost of living ...
>The *cost of living* is the expense of living in a country.
>The *standard of living* is how well you can live in a country.

... the level of local salaries.
>*Salaries* are normally paid monthly.
>*Wages* are normally paid weekly.

Neither have I.
>Note the word order after *neither*:
>*I didn't go to university. – Neither did I.*
>*I'm not going to move. – Neither am I.*
>
>*so* follows the same rule:
>*I studied in Moscow. – So did I.*
>*I'm moving to Tashkent. – So am I.*
>*I like working here. – So do I.*

... the company really looks after its people.
>Phrases for describing your employer:
>*It's a great/terrible company to work for.*
>*I have a very good/an awful boss.*

... I have free use of the company gym ...
>Some other benefits (if you are lucky!):
>*They pay for all my phone calls.*
>*I get excellent medical insurance.*
>*I have a good daily allowance.*

... promotion prospects are excellent.
>The speaker has a very good chance of getting a better paid job with more responsibility in the company.

How has the takeover affected the company?
>Note the use of the verb *to affect*.
>*How has the takeover affected you?* Compare:
>*What has been the effect of the takeover on the company?*

About 300 people are going to lose their jobs.
>This is more neutral than:
>*They are going to fire/sack fifty people.* or
>*Fifty people are going to be fired/sacked.*

... quite a few want to take early retirement.
>Note that we *take* early retirement. Other expressions:
>*I'd like to retire early.*
>*I'm not looking forward to retirement.*

... there are no compulsory redundancies.
>Note how we talk about *redundancy*:
>*Will anyone be made redundant?*
>*I was made redundant last year.*
>*Most of the redundancies will be voluntary.*

British/American differences

British	American
football team	soccer team
compulsory	mandatory
redundancies	layoffs
to be made redundant/to be laid off	to be laid off
I didn't go to university	I didn't go to college
I have a good daily allowance.	I have a good per diem.
To sack	to fire/dismiss (also used in British English)

Note: *To fire* is less formal than *to dismiss* in both British and American English.

Practice

1 Complete the missing word in the sentences and then put them in the grid. The letters in the tinted panel will spell a key word.

a You don't need to pay. Use of the gym is ..**free**......
b Is the cost of .... high in Norway?
c We need a person with .... communication skills.
d There is a good .... of nationalities in the office.
e Are you planning to take early ....?
f I understand some .... will be lost after the takeover.
g Do you know the .... of local salaries?
h My employer provides free .... insurance.

2 Complete the sentences with a form of the word in brackets.

EXAMPLE: John is now Head of .**recruitment**. (recruit)

a Because of the factory closure, 500 people are going to be made .... (redundancy)
b I'm in charge of .... (develop)
c The company provide free motor .... (insure)
d I'm planning to .... next year. (retirement)
e It is a very .... place to work. (stress)
f Do you know who the new .... of the company are? (own)
g We need a manager with excellent .... skills. (lead)
h I have good .... prospects in my new job. (promote)
i It's a very .... job. (challenge)
j It's a job with a wide range of .... (responsible)

3 Match the statements and questions with the responses.

1　I understand Frank used to work in Japan.
2　How are you?
3　I usually walk to work.
4　Did you have a good journey?
5　I don't have any regrets about moving.
6　Is it a good place to work?
7　Are you looking forward to retirement?
8　When did you graduate?
9　What time do you leave work?
10　We need someone who is very reliable.

a　Fine, thanks.
b　Yes, the directions were very clear.
c　At 4 p.m.
d　Yes, I am.
e　That's right, it was five years ago.
f　Neither do I.
g　It can be.
h　Absolutely!
i　So do I.
j　In 2001.

4 Complete the sentences with a preposition.

EXAMPLE: I'm in charge .... of ..... IT Services.

a　I'm responsible .... recruitment.
b　I report .... the Human Resources Director.
c　I take care .... everyday office procedures.
d　I studied .... my degree at Edinburgh University.
e　I have no regrets .... taking my current job.
f　Isn't the cost .... living very high?
g　I have free use .... the company swimming pool.

5 Complete the crossword.

Across
1　I work for a recruitment ....
3　I don't have time to eat in a restaurant at lunchtime. I usually have a ....
5　The meals in the staff .... are excellent.
7　I used to be paid .... , now I'm paid monthly.
8　I can't afford to live here. The .... of living is too high.

Down
2　She is an Oxford University ....
4　The company provides a very good daily .... for living expenses.
6　The company has changed enormously since the ....
9　'I'm moving to Istanbul next year.' 'Really? .... am I!'

31

6 Match the two parts of the sentences.

1 I graduated
2 I report
3 I studied
4 I go to work
5 We need to advertise
6 We offered her a salary of $60 000
7 The company looks
8 I'm looking forward

a for a degree in Business Administration.
b by car.
c plus commission.
d to early retirement.
e in the local newspaper.
f to the Chief Project Manager.
g after its staff well.
h from university five years ago.

7 Respond to the statements with *so* or *neither*.

EXAMPLE: I'm going to lose my job.
So am I.

a I didn't want to take early retirement.

b I went to University in France.

c I'm not going out this evening.

d I usually start at 8.00 a.m. in the morning.

e I don't like eating in the company canteen.

f I wasn't interested in my previous job.

g I was very happy in Thailand.

h I'm in the paper industry.

4 Presentations

**Some useful phrases.
Listen to the recording and repeat.**

I'm glad to see so many of you here today.
I'd like to talk about how we organise things in this department.
First I'll describe our organisation.
Finally, I'd like to discuss some future plans.

That's all I wanted to say about training.
Moving on to my next point …
Excuse me, can you tell us when the report will be ready?
Sorry, I didn't catch the question.
Could you bear with me?

Turnover rose by 12 per cent last year.
We are predicting a slowdown next year.
As you can see from the graph, sales have increased dramatically.
Sales reached a peak in December.
They have declined since then.
These are difficult times for the company.

I'd like to finish by thanking you all.
I'd welcome your feedback.

Dialogues 1

Setting the scene

A: Hello everyone. **It's good to see you all here** so early in the morning. My name's Hiro Rosado and **I'd like to talk about** how we organise language training here. **First I'll describe** how English has become the company language, then I'll outline our study programmes. Finally I'd like to say something about some of our plans for the future.

Moving on

A: ... so **that's all I wanted to say** about the budget for next year. I'd now like to move on to the question Rosa raised earlier.

... **That leads me to my next point.** We need to look carefully at how we plan for next year

... **So, next year's budget.** I'd now like to talk about the action we are taking to reach our targets.

Dealing with questions

A: How much is the project going to cost?
B: **I'm afraid I can't say** at the moment.
C: Can you tell us when the report will be ready?
B: I'm hoping to have it ready by the end of the week.
D: Are you planning to recruit more staff?
B: Sorry, **I didn't catch the question.** Could you repeat it, please?
D: Sorry, I'd like to know if you are planning to recruit more staff.
B: Did everyone hear that? The question was: 'Are we planning to recruit more staff?'

Dealing with the unexpected

A: Oh, dear.
B: Is it broken?
A: Yes, the bulb is broken. I'm afraid I won't be able to use the projector. **Could you bear with me,** I have some paper copies in my briefcase.
B: Are you OK?
A: Yes, I think so. Could I have a glass of water? That's better. **Sorry, where was I?**
B: **You were just about to tell us** some interesting news.

Recapping

A: **As I mentioned earlier,** we hope to finish the project by the end of the year. I said that we were on schedule. Having said that, there are a couple of potential problems ...

Coming to an end

A: **I'd like to finish by thanking you all** for coming here today and I look forward to seeing you in two weeks' time. If anyone has any questions, please ask. I will be around for coffee later and **you are very welcome to contact me** if you have any queries before the next meeting.

Notes

See the companion book in this series, *Business Presentations*, for more help with giving presentations in English.

It's good to see you all here ...
Speaker's opening remarks to an audience:
*I'm very pleased to be here.
I'm glad you could all make it.
Thanks for inviting me.
Thank you (all) for coming.*

... I'd like to talk about ...
Other common phrases for starting off a presentation:
*I'm planning to tell you about ...
Today I'd like to introduce ...
I'd like to start by saying something about ...*

First I'll describe ...
Phrases for describing the structure of a talk:
*Then I'll discuss our study programmes.
After that I'll come to the main point.
Finally I'd like to say something about ...*

... that's all I wanted to say ...
Note how the speaker finishes off a section of the talk. Some other phrases:
*Are there any questions so far?
Moving on to my next point ...
To summarise what I have said so far ...*

That leads me to my next point.
Announcing a new point in a presentation:
*I'd now like to move on Rosa's question.
Moving on to Rosa's question ...
Now I'd like to talk about ...*

So, next year's budget.
You can sometimes simply announce a new topic/presentation slide as follows:
*So, sales in Canada. These have been ...
Development plans for next year. These are ...
Study programmes. Have a look at ...*

I'm afraid I can't say ...
Useful language for when you do not know the answer to a question:
*I'm sorry, I don't know the answer.
I'll have to check for you.
I'm not the best person to answer that.
You need to speak to ...*

... I didn't catch the question.
When you can't hear something:
*Could you repeat the question?
Could you say that again?
Sorry, what did you say?*

Could you bear with me, ...
A very useful phrase when you need time to check or find something. Alternatives:
*Excuse me for a moment.
Just a moment.
Can you give me two minutes!*

Sorry, where was I?
If you are distracted or forget what you wanted to say! Other possibilities:
*Can you/anyone help me?
Let me think.*

You were just about to tell us ...
Helping the speaker to remember the point he/she wanted to make!
You were talking about the schedule.

As I mentioned earlier, ...
Useful language for recapping (summarising/reviewing) what was said earlier in the presentation:
*As I pointed out/mentioned earlier ...
As I said before ...*

I'd like to finish by thanking you all ...
Language for ending a talk:
*Thank you.
Thank you for inviting me.
Are there any questions?*

... you are very welcome to contact me ...
Asking the audience to contact you:
*I'd be very happy to hear from you.
I'd welcome your feedback.*

British/American differences

British	American
organise/organisation	organize/organization
study programmes	study programs
schedule	schedule
ˈʃedʒuːl, ˈskedjuːl	ˈskɛdʒəl, ˈskɛdʒul

Dialogues 2

Some facts and figures

A: Turnover rose in the year to April by 11 per cent to 4 billion dollars compared with 3.8 billion in the previous year. Profits jumped by 20 per cent in this period. However, these results give a misleading picture as the company sold its French subsidiary during the period for a 'one-off' profit of half a billion dollars.

Predictions

A: We're currently predicting a slow down in sales for next year. Global trading conditions are not promising. However, one area where we expect growth to continue is in Japan and Korea, where analysts are forecasting an upturn in the market.

B: Is that for the whole of the region?

A: Yes, we're looking at a growth rate of between 1 and 3 per cent in these areas.

Trends: upwards

A: As you can see from the graph, sales have increased considerably this year. The beginning of the year was poor, but sales picked up in February and reached a peak in August. Since then they have fallen a little but the overall trend is upwards. The outlook is very healthy.

Trends: downwards

A: The chart clearly shows the dramatic fall in production since the beginning of the year, and unfortunately this is a trend which will continue. The closure of our Lufwa plant in January accounts for the sharp fall at that time and as sales have continued to decline, we have had to temporarily shut down a number of our factories. These are difficult times for the company.

Trends: steady

A: If you compare this six-month period with the previous six months, you will notice that there has been very little change in the number of guests visiting our hotel. In fact, guest numbers have not increased for three years. We need to think about what we can do to make our hotel more popular.

Notes

Turnover rose in the year to April ...
Other ways of describing financial periods of time:
In the first/second/final quarter.
In the year to date.
In the current year.

... by 11 per cent ...
Note the use of the preposition *by* with percentages and fractions:
By what percentage did turnover grow?
It grew by 5.9%. (five point nine per cent)
... by 3.75%. (by three point seven five per cent)
It went up 2½%. (two and a half per cent)

... these results give a misleading picture ...
When information from charts and statistics is not so useful:
The graph gives a false picture.
The statistics may give you the wrong idea.

... a 'one-off' profit ...
A profit which will not be repeated.

We're currently predicting a slow down ...
Other ways to predict events:
We're forecasting an improvement.
We're expecting a sharp fall.

... analysts are forecasting an upturn ...
An *upturn* is a *recovery*.
A *downturn* is a *decline*.

... we're looking at a growth rate of between 1 and 3 per cent ...
to look at is an informal alternative expression meaning *to expect* or *to predict*:
We're looking at a large increase.
What kind of growth are we looking at next year?

As you can see from the graph, ...
Referring to visual aids:
This chart clearly shows the dramatic fall in production.
At this point on the graph you can see ...
Here you can see ...

... sales have increased considerably ...
Alternatives to *considerably*:
a lot, a great deal, substantially

... sales picked up in February ...
Other verbs to describe trends:
Sales recovered. (returned to their original level)
Turnover fell back. (declined)
Sales were up/down on last year. (better/worse than last year)

... sales reached a peak in August.
We can also say:
Sales reached their high/ highest point in August.
The opposite:
Sales reached their low/lowest point in June.

The closure of our Lufwa plant in January accounts for the sharp fall ...
To account for means to be the reason for. This is a useful term when talking about facts and figures.
How would you account for the fall in sales?
The appointment of a new Sales Manager accounts for the rapid rise in sales last year.
Note also *due to*:
The fall is due to the closure of the plant.

... sales have continued to decline ...
Further examples:
Sales have continued to fall.
There has been a further fall/decline in sales.

If you compare this six-month period ...
Note the use of a hyphen (-) in *six-month*.
Compare:
a three-month period
a period of three months

... there has been very little change ...
Note the use of the present perfect tense to describe change:
Things haven't changed very much.
Things have hardly changed.
Change has been very slight.
Sales have been steady.

British/American differences

British	American
a one-off profit	a one-shot/one-time profit
closure	closing

37

Practice

1 Complete the sentences with a preposition.

EXAMPLE: First I'd like to talk ..*about*.. how we organise training.

a Turnover increased .... more than ten per cent last year.

b Sales picked .... well in the first quarter of the year.

c Please bear .... me while I find the reference.

d We're forecasting an increase of .... two and three per cent.

e I'd like to finish .... thanking you all for your very useful comments.

f We are forecasting a downturn .... the market.

g Unfortunately, we had to shut .... our Luftwa plant earlier this year.

2 Write what you would say in these presentation situations. Refer to the dialogues and notes.

EXAMPLE: Start a talk. Explain what you are going to talk about.

Hello everyone. My name's Hiro Rosado and I'd like to talk about ...

a You are giving a presentation and someone asks you to go back to a previous slide. What could you say as you are looking for it?

....

b Invite questions from the audience.

....

c Refer to some details on a graph or chart.

....

d Finish the talk. Thank the audience.

....

3 Match the two parts of the sentences.

1	That leads me to	a	we hope to finish things soon.
2	As I mentioned earlier,	b	to contact me at any time.
3	You are welcome	c	so many of you here.
4	To summarise	d	there are some potential problems.
5	It's good to see	e	what I have said so far ...
6	Analysts are forecasting	f	a very healthy outlook for the company.
7	Excuse me	g	my main point ...
8	The graph compares	h	for a moment.
9	Having said that,	i	the number of guests visiting the hotel over a six-month period.

4 Write the phrases in one of the three columns depending if they are *up*, *down* or *the same*.

Up	Down	The same
Sales have picked up		

a Sales have picked up.
b There has been an increase in sales.
c Things are slowing down.
d Turnover jumped last year.
e It has stayed the same.
f Overall there has been a decline in the market.
g The company has recovered.
h We have seen a rise in turnover.
i There has been an upturn in the market.
j We are expecting a downturn.
k There has been little change.
l Sales have been steady during the year.

5 Complete the sentences with words used in the dialogues and notes.

EXAMPLE: I'm not the best . **person** . . . to answer that question.

a I didn't catch your . . . . Could you repeat it?
b Unfortunately the downward . . . . is going to continue.
c I'd like to make another . . . .
d The results give a misleading . . . . of last year's performance.
e What kind of growth . . . . are we hoping to achieve?
f We are very disappointed with the sharp . . . . in sales.
g Sales reached their highest . . . . in the summer.
h A lot has happened during the previous six-month . . . .

6 Complete the statements and questions using the verbs from the box. Use each verb once only.

| catch | repeat | show | account | take | |
| give | ~~cost~~ | say | fall | bear | |

EXAMPLE: I'd like to ask how much the project is going to . cost . . . . .

a   I'm afraid I can't . . . . I'll check for you.
b   I'm sorry I didn't . . . . the question.
c   Let me . . . . it for you.
d   I'm not quite ready. Can you . . . . with me?
e   Of course. . . . . your time.
f   I think these charts . . . . a false picture.
g   Yes, they don't really . . . . the recent upturn in the market.
h   By what percentage did turnover . . . . last year?
i   By 5 per cent. I can't . . . . for it.

7 Match the graphs with the descriptions.

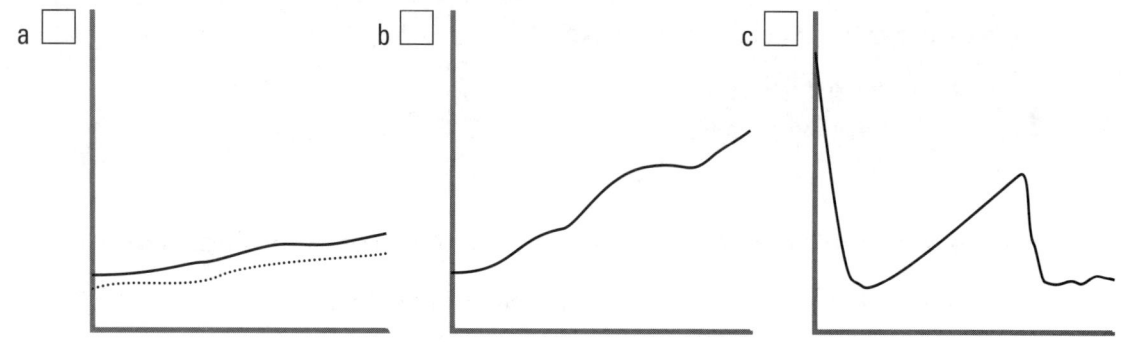

a ☐   b ☐   c ☐

1   The graph shows how sales have increased this year. Sales were very poor at the beginning of the year but they began to pick up in March and reached a peak in December. The outlook is very healthy.

2   This has been a difficult year for the company. As you can see, the chart shows the dramatic fall in production at the beginning of the year. Things began to improve but in June there was a serious fire in our factory and this accounts for the sharp fall in production at that time. The situation hasn't changed very much since then.

3   As you can see, we're looking at a growth rate of between 2 and 5 per cent in the three-month period, October to December. We're forecasting that this will be up on last year. We are quite happy with the situation.

5 Meetings

**Some useful phrases.
Listen to the recording and repeat.**

I'm trying to arrange a meeting for next week.
Can you make Thursday afternoon?
I don't think we need more than two hours.
I've booked the conference room for 2 o'clock.
I'll send you my draft proposals by Monday midday.

Who would like to take the minutes?
I'd like to leave item three until the next meeting.
What are your thoughts on this?
I'd like to make a point.
Of the fifty people I asked, only one did not agree with the idea.
Does everyone agree?

We made a very good case for changing the system.
Unfortunately they rejected nearly all of our proposals.
Only one of our proposals was accepted.

Here are the main points covered during the meeting.
I've attached the draft minutes of the meeting.
Please check if I have left anything out.
These are your action points.

Dialogues 1

Setting up a meeting (by phone)

A: Hi, Anna. I'm trying to arrange a meeting for next week. Can you make Tuesday or Thursday afternoon?
B: Tuesday would be fine. What time?
A: What about 3 o'clock? I don't think we need more than two hours.
B: I agree. Is Juan coming, by the way?
A: I hope so – but I haven't asked him yet.

Postponing a meeting (by phone)

A: Hello again. I hope this won't cause you any problems, but I've just spoken to Juan and he can't make Tuesday. Could we make it Thursday instead?
B: Just a moment. I'll just check my diary. Right, I've got another meeting on Thursday but it should be finished by 3:15. But, could we meet at 3:30 just in case the meeting overruns?
A: Of course. I know Juan will be pleased because he didn't want to miss the meeting.
B: Fine. See you on Thursday afternoon. I'll send you my draft proposals by Monday midday.
A: Thanks Anna. Bye.

Setting up a meeting (a voicemail message)

A: I'm sorry I can't take your call at the moment. Please leave your message after the tone and I'll get back to you as soon as I can.
B: Hello, Margaret, it's Dagmar here. I'd like to come over to Poznan next week to see you and Alex. There are some things we need to discuss relating to the arrangements for the conference. Any day next week except Friday would suit me. Could you check with Alex and get back to me? I think we'll need about three hours. Look forward to hearing from you.

Confirming a meeting by email

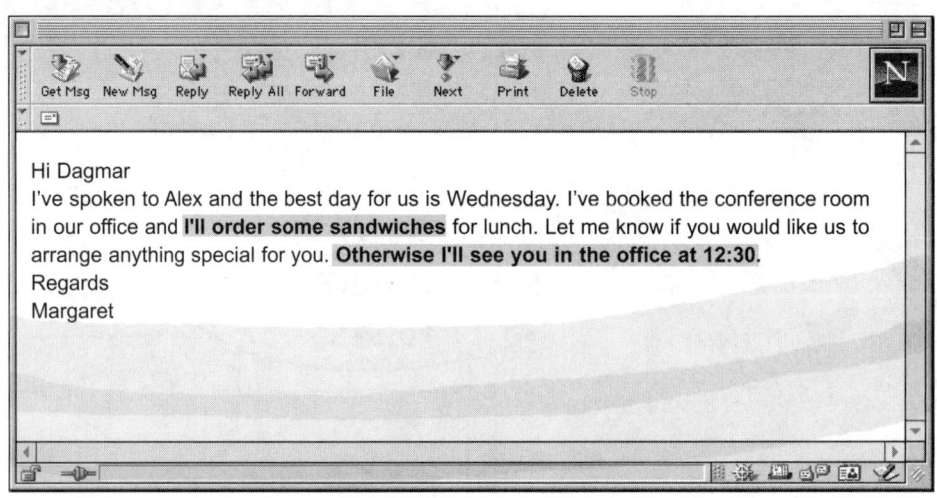

Hi Dagmar
I've spoken to Alex and the best day for us is Wednesday. I've booked the conference room in our office and I'll order some sandwiches for lunch. Let me know if you would like us to arrange anything special for you. Otherwise I'll see you in the office at 12:30.
Regards
Margaret

Notes

I'm trying to arrange a meeting for ...
Note the use of *for*:
... for next month.
... for next year.
... for the project group.

Can you make Tuesday?
This means *Can you come on Tuesday?*
Note the different uses of *make*:
Could we make it Thursday instead?
I could make it at 2 p.m.
I can't make the meeting.

Is Juan coming, by the way?
Use *by the way* to ask for additional information:
By the way, is anyone else coming?
Who else is coming, by the way?
We can also use *happen to*:
Do you happen to know if Juan is coming?

... it should be finished by 3:15.
Note that times can be said in two ways:
3:15 (a quarter past three or three fifteen)
3:20 (twenty past three or three twenty)
3:30 (half past three or three thirty)
3:45 (a quarter to four or three forty-five)
by 3:15 means that it could finish earlier
Compare:
at 3 o'clock (exactly 3 o'clock)
at around 3 o'clock (maybe a little earlier or later than 3 o'clock)
Note that *half three* in informal British English is 3:30.

... just in case the meeting overruns.
Another way of saying:
Just in case it doesn't finish on time.

... he didn't want to miss the meeting.
Note that *miss* has two meanings:
Unfortunately I had to miss the meeting.
I'm sorry I missed you earlier.
Compare with:
Juan is a very important member of the team – we really miss him when he is away.

I'd like to come over to Poznan next week ...
come over means travel from one place to another.
I'm thinking of coming over to visit.
You must come over and see the new office.

Any day next week except Friday would suit me.
Any day leaves the options open. The writer could have said:
I'm free every day next week except Friday.
That suits me means *That's a good time for me.*

Could you check with Alex and get back to me?
get back to me leaves the method of communication open; the contact could be by phone, email or letter.

... I'll order some sandwiches ...
Ordering sandwiches for a business lunch is not appropriate in all cultures! Some other useful lunch phrases:
Would you prefer to eat out?
Is there anything you don't eat?
Are you a vegetarian?
We can have a working lunch.
We often do business over lunch.

Otherwise I'll see you in the office at 12:30.
In this example, *otherwise* means *if I don't hear from you.*

British/American differences

British	American
Differences in time:	
a quarter past three or three fifteen	also: a quarter after three
a quarter to four or three forty-five	also: a quarter of four

Differences in dates:
British – 1/11/03 = 1 November 2003
(the first of November, two thousand and three)
American – 1/11/03 = January 11, 2003
(January eleventh, two thousand three)

Dialogues 2

Working through an agenda

- **A:** Has everyone got a copy of the agenda? Lee, could you take the minutes, please?
- **B:** No problem.
- **A:** Thanks. So, let's start. As we're rather short of time today, I'd like to leave item four until the next meeting. Is that OK with everyone?
- **B:** That's fine with me.
- **A:** Good, so can we look at item one? That's John's proposal that future department team meetings should be held away from the office. What are your thoughts on this?

Reporting back to a meeting

- **A:** John, could you give us your report?
- **B:** Certainly. As you know, I was asked to find out what the people in my department thought about arranging more meetings away from the office. I found that most of my staff were opposed to the idea. The majority feeling was that they would prefer to organise meetings in this building.
- **A:** That's interesting. Sandra, what did you find out?
- **C:** Quite the opposite. In my department, of the fifty people I asked, only five did not like the idea of having meetings away from the office.

Reaching an agreement

- **A:** I think we should abandon the idea altogether. Does everyone agree?
- **B:** Not really. I think we need to send a questionnaire to all the staff so we can find out exactly what they think.
- **C:** Is that really necessary? You've heard what John and Sandra have said – there are so many different views. It's not worth it.
- **A:** I suppose you're right. It just seemed like a good idea to me.
- **B:** It is a good idea. Perhaps we could look at it again next year!

Making a point

- **A:** The other point I want to make is that we need to be informed about the dates of meetings well in advance. I was told about the date of this meeting very late and that caused me a lot of problems. Some people were not able to come at all. We really must avoid this in the future. Communication is very bad in this company.
- **B:** That's not true. Some people simply do not read their messages. The date was set three weeks ago and everyone was told then.

Notes

... could you take the minutes, please?
> The *minutes* are the written record of what is discussed during a meeting.
> The *agenda* is the list of items discussed in a meeting.
> Minutes are *taken* during a meeting.
> The minutes of a meeting can be *written up* and *approved*.

... I'd like to leave item four until the next meeting.
> We usually talk about *items* or *points* on an agenda.

... can we look at item one?
> Note that we can look *at* an item on the agenda. Some other useful verbs and prepositions:
> Let's move <u>on to</u> item two <u>on</u> the agenda.
> Can we go <u>through</u> the minutes?
> We need to vote on it.

What are your thoughts on this?
> Asking for opinions:
> How do you feel about this?
> What do you think?
> I'd like to hear everyone's opinion.

... I was asked to find out what the people in my department thought ...
> Reporting back:
> It was my job to find out about ...
> You asked me to find out about ...
> I've talked to the office staff and the general opinion is ...

The majority feeling was ...
> Majority opinions:
> Most people are in favour of the change.
> The majority opinion is in favour.
> Minority opinions:
> Not many people agree with the idea.
> The minority opinion is against it.

British/American differences	
British	**American**
favour	favor
emphasise	emphasize

... of the fifty people I asked, only five ...
> More numbers and percentages:
> One in fifty agreed with the idea.
> Two in three are against it.
> Nearly 100 per cent of the staff replied to the questionnaire.
> A quarter/Half/Three quarters of the staff were in favour.

Does everyone agree?
> Ways to find out if there is agreement:
> Are we all in agreement?
> Do you have the same opinion?
> Does anyone disagree?

Is that really necessary?
> *really* is used more in spoken English to emphasise what you are saying:
> Are you really sure?
> Is he really leaving the company?
> They really don't want to leave the office.

I suppose you're right.
> The speaker uses *suppose* to admit that the other speaker is, in fact, right.

The other point I want to make ...
> Some alternative expressions:
> I'd like to make another point.
> Just one other point ...
> I'd like to make one final point.

We really must avoid this in the future.
> Making a strong statement:
> It's vital that we avoid this in the future.
> It's essential that we make changes.
> It's crucial that people should read their messages.

That's not true.
> Note that this is a very direct statement and could be considered impolite. Less direct alternatives:
> I'm sorry, but I don't agree.
> I don't think that's true.
> I'm not sure that's true.
> Is that really true?

Dialogues 3

A follow-up phone call (1)

A: Hi, Kitty. I'm just phoning to let you know what happened in the meeting.
B: Thanks. So how did it go?
A: Bad news I'm afraid. They rejected all of our proposals to change suppliers to AKK. Some of the managers agreed that we needed to change but Anton Trofimov persuaded them to leave things as they are.
B: So what reasons did he give?
A: Anton said he thought that the current arrangements were 'good enough' and finally everyone else agreed with him.
B: I don't believe it. How can they be so short-sighted?

A follow-up phone call (2)

A: Hello again, Kitty. I thought I should let you know immediately that Anton has been having second thoughts. He's been through the figures which I presented at the meeting again and he now thinks we've made a good case for moving our business over to AKK.
B: Do you want me to do anything?
A: No, but thanks for offering. Anton would like me to provide some more information about AKK at another meeting to be held next week. I'll call you tomorrow so we can discuss details then.
B: Fine. Speak to you then.

Action points (on a dictaphone)

Here are the main points covered during the meeting on February 14th and action to be taken.
- Jaroslav to produce a questionnaire to find out how the staff would like to spend the 'New Year bonus'.
- Juliet to research costs for proposed building project.
- Winston to look into improving our security systems.
- Tree planting project – no decision made. Leave until the next meeting.

The next meeting will be on March 3rd.

Sending minutes by email

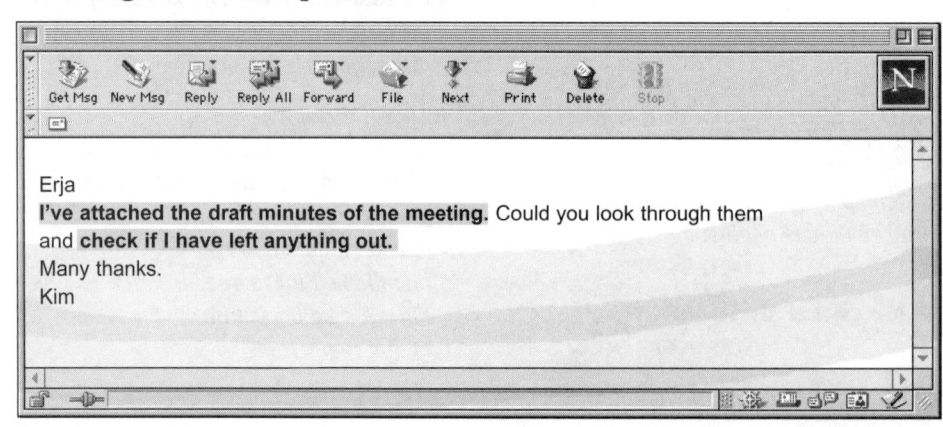

Erja
I've attached the draft minutes of the meeting. Could you look through them and check if I have left anything out.
Many thanks.
Kim

Notes

I'm just phoning to let you know …
    Announcing the reason for a call:
    I'm just phoning to say thank you for doing the minutes.
    I'm just calling to remind you about next week's meeting.

Bad news I'm afraid.
    The speaker says *bad news* at the beginning of the sentence for emphasis. He could also have said:
    I'm afraid I have some bad news.
    Other examples:
    Good news, I'm happy to say.
    I'm happy to say I have some good news.

… what reasons did he give?
    Note the use of *give*:
    to give a reason/reasons
    to give an explanation/explanations

… short-sighted.
    When you only think about the present, not the future.

I thought I should let you know immediately …
    You can also say *I wanted to* instead of *I thought* in this situation:
    I wanted to let you know what happened.

… Anton has been having second thoughts.
    to have second thoughts means to change your opinion after you have thought about it again.
    Are you having second thoughts?
    On second thoughts, I'd like to accept the proposal.

… he now thinks we've made a good case …
    The speaker uses the word *now* to show that he has changed his mind.

British/American differences	
British	**American**
Bad news I'm afraid.	*There's bad news.* (Also used in British English.)
On second thoughts …	*On second thought …*

I'll call you tomorrow so we can discuss details then.
    I will call is usually reduced to *I'll call* in spoken English. It implies a promise/a firm arrangement:
    I'll let you know.
    I'll send you a message.
    I'll organise it., etc.

Here are the main points …
    We can start the memo with *Here are …* or simply use the following:
    The main points.
    Action points.

Jaroslav to produce a questionnaire …
    Note the use of the infinitive *to* in these statements. This is very common when writing informal action points from a meeting:
    Juliet to research costs for the proposed building project.
    Winston to look into improving our security systems.

… for proposed building project.
    Note how the article *the* (for the proposed project) can be left out when the memo is in note form.

… no decision made.
    No decision was made.
    Auxiliary verbs (*was* in this example) can be left out when you write/speak in note form.

I've attached the draft minutes of the meeting.
    Alternatives:
    The draft minutes are attached.
    Herewith the draft minutes. (more formal)
    Drafts can be *first drafts*, *rough drafts* or *final drafts*.

… check if I have left anything out.
    Other possibilities:
    Let me know if I have forgotten anything.
    Check if I have made any mistakes.

Practice

1 Complete the sentences using the verbs from the box below.
Use each verb once only.

| ~~arrange~~ | cover | miss | cause | make |
| give | report | happen | leave | abandon |

EXAMPLE: I'd like to ...*arrange*... a meeting for next week.

a Can you .... the meeting on Tuesday?
b I hope that the changed time won't .... you any problems.
c I must hurry. I don't want to .... the meeting.
d Do you .... to know if Motoko is going to be there?
e I don't like it all. We should .... the idea.
f Let's .... discussion on this point until the next meeting.
g I'll talk to the staff and .... back to you next week.
h Did Tonya .... a reason why she couldn't attend?
i We have a lot of things to .... in this meeting.

2 Complete the sentences with words taken from the dialogues.
The first letter of each word is provided.

a The   m................ of the staff were in favour.
b Can we look at the first   i................ on the agenda?
c Is it   n................ to send an agenda beforehand?
d I'd like to leave point two   *until*............ the next meeting.
e Can we go   t................ the report now?
f I can meet any day next week   e................ Monday.
g Does Tuesday   s................ you?

3 Complete the sentences with one of the alternatives.

EXAMPLE: I'm phoning to . *let* .... you know what happened.   let/explain

a Who is going to .... the minutes?   make/take
b Could you .... us when you know the answer.   tell/say
c I'd like to .... a point.   make/remind
d We need to .... a date for the meeting.   take/set
e We .... a good case for changing the system.   made/took
f Are you .... second thoughts about the proposal?   having/taking
g All of our proposals were ....   disagreed/rejected

48

4 Complete the sentences with a preposition.

EXAMPLE: The meeting should be finished ..by.. 3 p.m.

a   I booked the room . . . . . . 1 p.m.
b   I'll see you . . . . . . Thursday at 11 o'clock.
c   I'd like to hear everyone's thoughts . . . . . . the proposal.
d   . . . . . . the ten people I asked, only one was against the idea.
e   It seems like a good idea . . . . . . me.
f   Can we move . . . . . . to the next item . . . . . . the agenda?
g   Most of the participants were . . . . . . favour of the suggestion.
h   One . . . . . . twenty of the staff are unhappy with working conditions.
i   Could you look . . . . . . the minutes and let me know if I've forgotten anything.
j   I hope I haven't left anything . . . .

5 Write what you would say in these situations. Refer to the dialogues and notes.

EXAMPLE: Check that everyone has a copy of the agenda.

   Has everyone *got a copy of the agenda?* . . . . ?

a   Suggest leaving the next item on the agenda until the next meeting.
   I'd like . . . .

b   Ask if everyone agrees that date of the next meeting should be changed.
   Does everyone . . . . ?

c   Ask Fiona if she is going to attend the next meeting.
   Are you . . . . ?

d   Call a colleague to tell him/her what happened in the meeting.
   I'm just phoning . . . .

e   Tell a colleague that you are sending the agenda as an email attachment.
   I've . . . .

f   Say that you have one more point to make.
   Just . . . .

g   Ask what people think about the idea.
   What . . . . ?

6 Match the two parts of the sentences.

1. I'd like to leave point three
2. The majority feeling
3. You've all heard
4. Very few people
5. Bad news
6. I'll call you tomorrow
7. Could you check the dates
8. If I don't hear from you,
9. Any day except Thursday

a are in favour of the changes.
b and we can discuss details then.
c is that people want to work shorter hours.
d I'll expect to see you at 2 p.m.
e what Maria has said about this.
f until the next meeting.
g suits me.
h I'm afraid.
i and get back to me.

7 Complete the sentences with a form of the verb in brackets. Refer to the dialogues and notes.

EXAMPLE: Hi, John. *I'm trying* .... (try) to arrange a meeting for next week.

a I hope it .... (not cause) you any problems if we postpone the meeting.

b I .... (order) some sandwiches for lunch.

c I'm sorry I .... (miss) the last meeting.

d I .... (see) you in the conference room at 3 p.m.

e .... (everyone/agree) with the proposals? Good, then let's move on.

f Hello, Anton. I .... (call) to let you know what happened in the meeting.

g I don't think that Margaret .... (read) the report.

h Memo: Frieda .... (find out) about tree planting costs.

i I .... (attach) the minutes from the last meeting.

j I .... (have) second thoughts about your proposals.

6 Entertaining and socialising

**Some useful phrases.
Listen to the recording and repeat.**

Would you like tea or coffee?
How do you like your coffee?
Can I have a soft drink?

Could you translate the menu for me, please?
Do you have an English menu?
We're ready to order.
That was delicious.
Can I have the bill please?

So where do you live?
In a small town not far from Milan.
Did you watch the match on TV last night?
Where are you going for your holidays this year?
We're planning to go to Italy.

I've been invited to dinner with the Managing Director this evening.
I'd like to take a small present. Do you have any suggestions?
I'm sure she'd like some flowers.

It's a formal dinner.
We're having an informal reception.

I TOLD THEM WE WERE HAVING AN INFORMAL RECEPTION BY THE HOTEL POOL.

Dialogues 1

Coffee or tea?

- Ⓐ: Would you like some coffee?
- Ⓑ: Do you have any tea?
- Ⓐ: Yes, we do. Do you take milk and sugar?
- Ⓑ: No thanks.
- Ⓒ: Can I have a soft drink, please?
- Ⓐ: Yes, of course. We have some orange juice and some sparkling water.
- Ⓒ: I'll have an orange juice, please.

Translating the menu

- Ⓐ: I hope you like Russian food. Let me translate the menu for you. I recommend the set menu which is 'borsch' – that's beetroot soup, followed by 'buglama', which is a kind of lamb stew cooked in spices – it comes with mashed potato and salad.
- Ⓑ: Sounds good. What about dessert?
- Ⓐ: There's a choice of ice cream.
- Ⓑ: I'm happy with that. Let's order.

Ordering a meal (1)

- Ⓐ: We're ready to order. To start, I'd like chicken soup and my colleague would like the grilled sardines.
- Ⓑ: Thank you. And for your main course?
- Ⓐ: I'd like fried chicken and French fries and, was it roast duck and boiled rice?
- Ⓒ: That's right. With a green side salad, please.
- Ⓑ: Thank you. And to drink?
- Ⓐ: We'd like a bottle of sparkling water, please?

Ordering a meal (2)

- Ⓐ: Are you ready to order?
- Ⓑ: Yes please. I'd like the steak, please.
- Ⓐ: How would you like it cooked?
- Ⓑ: Medium rare.
- Ⓐ: Thank you. Are you having a starter?
- Ⓑ: No thanks. I'm in rather a hurry.

Paying the bill

- Ⓐ: That was very good. Can we have the bill, please?
- Ⓑ: Here you are, sir.
- Ⓐ: Excuse me, but could you tell me what this is for?
- Ⓑ: It's for the bread.
- Ⓐ: Oh yes, I see. Do you take credit cards?
- Ⓑ: I'm sorry, we don't. If you need some cash, there's a cash machine just across the road.

Notes

Would you like some coffee?
You can also ask if someone would like a drink or snack by using the word with rising intonation:
More coffee? Tea? Sugar? Milk?

Do you take milk and sugar?
Also note:
How do you like your coffee?
Just a little milk, please.
Help yourself to milk and sugar.
No milk for me, thanks.

Can I have a soft drink, please?
Soft drinks are non-alcoholic drinks:
fruit juices include *orange juice, apple juice, grapefruit juice*
I'd prefer water.
Would you like sparkling or still water?

Let me translate the menu for you.
When you need a translation:
Could you translate the menu?
What's that in Italian?
Do you have an English menu?

… 'Borsch', that's beetroot soup, …
Language for explaining the menu:
It's a speciality of this region.
Would you like to try one of the 'specials'?
It's a kind of soup.
It tastes like chicken.
It's delicious. I recommend it.

We're ready to order.
Or the waiter/waitress can say:
Are you ready to order?
Can I take your order?

And for your main course?
Stages of a meal:
I don't really want a starter.
Can I see the dessert menu?
Thank you. That was very good/delicious.

I'd like fried chicken …
Some methods of cooking:
roast (roast duck, roast beef)
boiled (boiled rice, boiled potatoes)
steamed (steamed vegetables, steamed fish)
grilled (grilled sardines)

Medium rare.
Other ways of cooking steak:
rare, medium, well done

Can we have the bill please?
The waiter might ask:
Would you like anything else?
Possible replies:
No, just the bill, please.
Another coffee, please.

Excuse me, but could you tell me what this is for?
Asking about the bill:
Sorry, I don't understand the bill.
Is service included?
We ordered one salad but you've charged us for two.

Do you take credit cards?
Other useful phrases:
Can I pay by card?
How much do you normally tip? (not a question we usually ask the waiter!)

… there's a cash machine just across the road.
A *cash machine, cash dispenser* or *cash point* (UK) = an ATM (Automatic Teller Machine) (US)

British/American differences

British	American
Do you take milk and sugar?	Do you use milk and sugar?
beetroot soup	beet soup
mashed potato	mashed potatoes
Can I have the bill please?	Can I have the check please?
a starter	an appetizer
Is service included?	Is the gratuity included?

Phrases for beginning meals:
There is no special phrase in English for starting a meal. If something is said, it might be *bon appetit* or, informally, *Let's start*. If wine is served, *Cheers* or *To your health* can be used.

Dialogues 2

Where you live

- **A:** Where do you live, Xavier?
- **B:** In Sitges, near Barcelona.
- **A:** Oh, I know Barcelona very well. It's one of my favourite cities.
- **B:** And mine. Sitges is a beautiful little town just along the coast from Barcelona. I've lived there all my life. It's a great place for a holiday but best to go out of season.

Starting a conversation

- **A:** Did you see the football match last night?
- **B:** Yes, I did. I thought Owen played very well.
- **A:** So did I. I thought his first goal was fantastic. So you like football, do you?
- **B:** I quite like it. I watch international matches and I follow my local team, but I prefer basketball.

Family matters

- **A:** Where are you going for your summer holiday?
- **B:** I'm going to the French Alps with the family. We all want to do different things, so it's a great place for us. My son and daughter can go mountain biking, and my partner and I can go walking and play some golf.
- **A:** How old are your children?
- **B:** Eleven and thirteen. What about you? Do you have any children?
- **A:** Yes, but they're all grown up. They don't want to come on holiday with us any more.

Cultural advice

- **A:** I've been invited to dinner with Paulo and Maria this evening but I don't know what to wear. I'd also like to take a small present. Do you have any suggestions?
- **B:** Just be casual. I'm sure they'd appreciate some flowers and maybe something from Scotland.
- **A:** I've got a box of Scottish biscuits with me.
- **B:** That would be fine.

Sensitive issues

- **A:** I'm looking forward to meeting David this afternoon.
- **B:** Oh, haven't you heard? He's left the company.
- **A:** I'm sorry to hear that. What happened? I thought he was doing very well with you.
- **B:** He was, but there were a few problems. I'm afraid I can't really go into it now.
- **A:** I understand. Tell me another time.

Notes

Where do you live, Xavier?
Note how English speakers often use a person's first name to be friendly and engaging. Note, however, that this is not appropriate in all cultures.

Oh, I know Barcelona very well.
A typical expression/response for keeping a conversation going – some other possibilities:
Oh, I've been there.
Really? What's it like?
Lucky you!
That's a nice place to live.

It's a great place for a holiday ...
Some other ways of recommending (and not recommending) somewhere for a holiday:
I always spend my summer holidays there.
You must go there.
I wouldn't recommend it.
It isn't a good place for a holiday.

Did you see the football match last night?
Not everyone likes football! Some other ways to open a conversation:
How was the weather when you left home?
Have you seen any good films recently?
Have you bought any souvenirs?

So you like football, do you?
Note the use of the 'question tag' for engaging the other speaker:
Terrible weather, isn't it?
You're working next week, aren't you?
Liz is coming this evening, isn't she?

Where are you going for your summer holiday?
Keeping the conversation going:
Do you travel a lot on business?
What are you doing at the weekend?
What are your first impressions of the town?

My son and daughter can go mountain biking, ...
Note some verbs which go with sports:
go biking/swimming/riding
play tennis/golf/football
do gymnastics/weightlifting

Do you have any children?
Talking about your relatives:
My uncle/aunt worked for the company.
My niece/nephew lives in Canada.
My cousin is getting married next year.

... I don't know what to wear.
Some advice:
It's very informal.
Wear something casual.
You'll need to wear a collar and tie.
What you're wearing is fine.

I'm sure they'd appreciate some flowers ...
They'd appreciate ... means They'd really like ...

I'm sorry to hear that.
Other possible responses:
Really?
That's a shame!
I don't believe it!

... I can't really go into it now.
When you would prefer not to say anything:
Sorry, but I don't really want to talk about it.
Do you mind if I tell you later?
Can we talk about it later?

I understand.
A useful response to demonstrate that the speaker is happy to be told the news another time. Alternatively:
No problem!

British/American differences

British	American
football match	soccer game
summer holiday	summer vacation
a box of biscuits	a package of cookies
You'll need to wear a collar and tie.	You'll need to wear a shirt and tie.

Practice

1 Write what you would you say in these situations. Refer to the dialogues and notes.

   EXAMPLE: Tell the waiter/waitress that you would like to order your meal.

   ...We're ready to order. / We'd like to order...........

   a You don't understand the menu written in Turkish. Ask a colleague for help.
   ....

   b Order something to eat in a restaurant.
   ....

   c Ask for the bill.
   ....

   d Check an item on the bill that you do not understand.
   ....

   e Ask a business acquaintance where he/she lives.
   ....

   f Say something about where you live.
   ....

   g Say something about your holiday plans for the year.
   ....

   h You hear that a business contact has left the company. What do you say?
   ....

2 Complete the sentences with a preposition.

   EXAMPLE: How do you say that .... *in* ...... English?

   a What would you like .... your main course?
   b The grilled chicken comes .... fried potatoes.
   c Help yourselves .... salad.
   d Can I pay .... credit card?
   e Sydney is a great place .... a holiday.
   f Where are you going .... holiday this year?
   g I can't really go .... detail now.
   h Can we talk .... it later?

3 Complete the phrases 1–8 with the verbs in the box and match them with a–h to make questions.

accept	wear	have	take	see	happened	watch	know

1 Can I . have   a to David? Is he OK?
2 Do you . . . . all   b the basketball game yesterday?
3 Do you . . . . if there is   c the dessert menu?
4 Do you . . . .   d credit cards?
5 Would anyone like to . . . . e sugar in your coffee?
6 Did you . . . .   f to the reception?
7 What clothes should I . . . . g a cash machine nearby?
8 What has . . . .   h the chicken and vegetable soup, please?

4 Complete the dialogue. Choose from the phrases in the box below.

a I wasn't surprised	e Sarah is leaving the company next month
b So, what's happening at work	f Yes, I heard that
c I thought she really enjoyed her job	g How are things
d Fine, thanks	h Really

A: Hi Nigel. ① . . . . ?

B: ② . . . . ③ . . . . ?

A: Some sad news I'm afraid. ④ . . . .

B: ⑤ . . . .

A: I couldn't believe it. ⑥ . . . .

B: ⑦ . . . . ? ⑧ . . . .

5 Choose an appropriate response.

1   Do you have any turkey?   a Yes, I did.
2   Do you take sugar?   b It's a kind of bread.
3   And for your main course?   c I understand.
4   Excuse me, what's this for?   d It's a service charge.
5   And what would you like to drink?   e Tea, please.
6   How would you like it cooked?   f I'm very sorry, we don't.
7   Did you play golf yesterday?   g I'll have the chicken.
8   I can't really discuss this now.   h Not really.
9   Would you recommend Elohlleh for a holiday? i I'd like it fried.
10 What's a 'tortilla'?   j No, thanks.

6 Which of the following sports and activities go with the verbs *play* and *go*. Look the words up in a dictionary if you do not know them.

| walking | golf | tennis | climbing | badminton | volleyball | hiking |
| basketball | diving | snorkelling | ping pong | cycling | sailing |

play ....

go ....

7 Complete the sentences using the words in the box.

| niece | nephew | aunt | cousin | uncle |

a   My brother's son is my ....

b   My mother's sister is my ....

c   My brother's son is my daughter's ....

d   My father's brother is my ....

e   My sister's daughter is my ....

8 Put the dialogue in the right order.

a   What are you going to do while you're there?

b   Why Hereford?

c   It's a beautiful part of the world

d   Where are you going

e   To the UK.

f   and we have some friends who live there.

g   We're staying in a small hotel in Hereford.

h   for your holiday this year?

I   We're planning to do some walking

j   and there are some excellent places to eat.

k   Maybe next year.

l   You must go there.

d, h, e,..

7 Travel

**Some useful phrases.
Listen to the recording and repeat.**

I'd like an aisle seat, please.
I'd like to sit next to my colleague.
I only have one bag to check in.

I'd like to book a hire car for three days.
Do I need an international driving licence?
How would you like to pay?
Do you take credit cards?

A single to Munich, please.
Do I need to reserve a seat?
Is the seat reservation included in the price of the ticket?

Do you have a double room for two nights?
A non-smoking room please, with a bath and a balcony.
We need your credit card number to hold the reservation.

I'm calling from room 21.
The TV doesn't work.
The bed hasn't been made.
I'd like to change my room.

I don't have any cash on me.
That's OK. You can pay by credit card.

🔊 Dialogues 1

Checking in for a flight

- **A:** Can I have your ticket and passport, please? Thank you. **Would you like an aisle or a window seat?**
- **B:** I'd like an aisle seat if possible.
- **A:** OK. I have given you a seat in the exit row. Is that all right?
- **B:** Yes, that's fine. Thanks. And I'd like to sit next to my colleague if possible.
- **A:** I'm sorry. We don't have any more seats together. Could you talk to the cabin attendant when you board the plane?

Hiring a car

- **A:** Hello, **I'd like to book a hire car** for three days from March 14th –17th, please. Do I need an international driving licence to drive here?
- **B:** No, but there is a charge for an extra driver.
- **A:** So how much will it cost in total?
- **B:** $300. **How would you like to pay?**
- **A:** By credit card, please.

Taking the train

- **A:** **A single to Munich, please.**
- **B:** First or second class?
- **A:** First class, please.
- **B:** OK. That will be 70 euros. Please sign here.
- **A:** **Do I need to reserve a seat?**
- **B:** No, the seat reservation is included in the price.

Booking a hotel

- **A:** Wellington Hotel. Can I help you?
- **B:** Yes, I've been trying to book a room on your hotel website but I can't complete the booking.
- **A:** Sorry, sir. I can do the booking for you.
- **B:** Thank you. **I'd like to book a twin room** for two nights, the 12th and 13th of June.
- **A:** Just one moment. I'll check our availability. Can I have your name please?
- **B:** Yes, it's Cook. **I won't be arriving until 11:00 p.m.** Do you need my credit card number to hold the reservation?
- **A:** Yes, please.

Checking into a hotel

- **A:** Hello, **I have a reservation in the name of Perry.**
- **B:** I'm sorry, I cannot find a booking in that name. Did you book the room yourself?
- **A:** No, my company, Carditis, booked it.
- **B:** Ah yes, here it is. **Could you fill in this form, please?** Would you like a smoking or non-smoking room?
- **A:** A non-smoking room, please, with a bath and a balcony if possible.
- **B:** We have a non-smoking room with a balcony on the 10th floor. Enjoy your stay.

Notes

Would you like an aisle or a window seat?
Seating preferences:
I'd prefer an aisle seat.
I don't really want a middle seat.
Do you have a seat in the exit row?
I'd like to change my seat.

... I'd like to book a hire car ...
Useful phrases when you need to hire a car:
Is there a charge for an extra driver?
Does it include insurance?
Where do I return the car?
Do you need my driving licence?

How would you like to pay?
Other language for making payments:
How do you want to pay?
Are you paying by cheque/credit/debit card?
I'd prefer to pay in cash.

A single to Munich, please.
Useful language at the ticket office:
I'd like a first class return to London, please.
Which platform do I need?
Is there a buffet car?

Do I need to reserve a seat?
More language for making reservations:
Do I need to book in advance?
Are seat reservations compulsory?
I'd like a forward/backward-facing seat.
Will the train be crowded?

I'd like to book a twin room ...
Some hotel room options:
A double/single room.
A quiet room with a good view.
A suite with a balcony.
An en suite room. (a room with a separate bathroom)
A shared bathroom.

I won't be arriving until 11:00 p.m.
Alternatively we can say:
I hope to be there by 11:00 p.m.
I'm hoping to arrive by 11:00 p.m.
I should be there by 11:00 p.m.

... I have a reservation in the name of Perry.
When you arrive at the hotel, you can say:
My name is (Mr Perry).
Do you have a reservation for a (Mr Perry)?
The reservation was made by my company.

Could you fill in this form, please?
Some hotels might not ask you to fill in a form:
I just need your passport.
Just sign here, please.

British/American differences

British	American
a hire car	a rental car
a non-smoking room	a no-smoking room
a double/single room	Note: hotels in the US use varying terminology but these are usual:

a single = room with one double bed
a double = a room with two double beds
a queen = a room with one queen size bed
a king = a room with one king size bed

an ensuite room	Note: this phrase is not used in American English.

We have a non-smoking room with a balcony on the 10th floor.
Note that the 10th floor in the UK would be the 11th floor in the US.
UK *Ground floor*   US *First floor*
UK *First floor*   US *Second floor*

I just need to see your passport.
Americans usually use their driver's license or a special ID card for identification

Other useful travel vocabulary
Platform 1   *Track 1*
Single ticket   *One-way ticket*
Return ticket   *Round trip*
Underground   *Subway*

Some UK – US spelling differences:
driving licence/driving license, centre/center, cheque/check, colour/color, theatre/theater, traveller/traveler, favour/favor, defence/defense, fulfil/fulfill, practise (verb)*/practise* (verb and noun)

Dialogues 2

At the check-in desk

A: Can I see your hand luggage, please?
B: I just have this bag and a laptop.
A: Could you put them on the scales? I'm afraid the bag will have to go in the hold.
B: Is that really necessary? It's very small.
A: I'm afraid so.

A flight delay

A: I'm sorry Carmen, but I'm not going to get to the meeting on time. There was a delay coming into the airport and I've just missed my connection. If I'm lucky, I'll get a seat on the flight that leaves in half an hour.
B: Don't worry, as long as you're here for the afternoon session, it doesn't matter too much.
A: Thanks. I'll let you know if I don't manage to catch the flight, otherwise expect to see me about 12:30 – in time for lunch.

A tight connection

A: Excuse me. I have a connection to Chicago at 5:00. Am I going to make it?
B: Yes, there will be a minibus waiting at the gate to take you to terminal B. There shouldn't be a problem.
A: What about my luggage? I'm worried that my bags won't make the connection even if I do.
B: Don't worry, the minibus will take you and your luggage. There are some other passengers who also have tight connections.
A: Thanks for your help. I'll keep my fingers crossed.

A hotel mix-up

A: Hello, Reception.
B: Hello, it's Amanda Lin from Room 205. I asked for a non-smoking room but someone has been smoking in this room. Oh yes, and the TV doesn't work. Also there are no drinks in the minibar and the bed hasn't been made. I'd like to change rooms.
A: I'm very sorry, madam. I'll organise a different room for you and send someone up immediately to help you with your luggage.

A payment problem

A: I'm sorry but we need some identification if you'd like to pay by credit card.
B: Oh, I don't think I have any identification with me and I don't have enough cash. I'm sure I paid by credit card last time I was here.
A: Yes, we do accept credit cards but only if the bill is under 100 euros. I'm afraid it's a security rule.
B: I understand. Can I pay 100 euros with my card and the rest in cash?
A: Yes, that would be fine.

Notes

I just have this bag and a laptop.
> *just* means *only* in this example. Other examples:
> *I just need five minutes.*
> *I just need to check your visa.*

... the bag will have to go in the hold.
> Problems with hand luggage:
> *It can go under my seat.*
> *Can I put it in the overhead lockers?*
> *It's too large to go in the cabin.*
> *It's fragile.*

... I'm not going to get to the meeting on time.
> *On time* means exactly on time.
> Compare:
> *I'll be there in time for lunch.* (just before lunch)
> *I won't be there in time for Petra's talk.* (but I will be there)

... I've just missed my connection.
> Catching another flight:
> *When's the next flight?*
> *Where is the check-in desk?*
> *How far is it to the gate?*

I'll let you know if I don't manage to catch the flight, ...
> Notice how we can use *manage*:
> *I just managed to catch the flight.*
> *I hope you manage with all your luggage – it looks heavy.*
> *Can you manage? Can I help you?*

... there will be a minibus waiting at the gate ...
> Making sure you catch the flight:
> *I'm worried I won't make the connection.*
> *Are you sure I'll make it?*
> *You'll have to hurry.*

I'll keep my fingers crossed.
> If you want to wish someone else good luck say:
> *Fingers crossed!*
> *Good luck!*

I asked for a non-smoking room ...
> Other complaints:
> *The TV doesn't work.*
> *The air-conditioning doesn't work.*
> *It's very smoky in the room.*
> *The room is very dusty/dirty/noisy.*

... the bed hasn't been made.
> Note the use of the present perfect passive:
> *The room hasn't been cleaned.*
> *The bins haven't been emptied.*
> Compare with the simple past passive:
> *The room was cleaned this morning.*
> *The bins weren't emptied yesterday.*

... we need some identification ...
> Some responses:
> *What kind of identification do you need?*
> *I don't have my passport on me.*
> *I've left my documents behind.*

... I don't have enough cash.
> Problems:
> *I've only got twelve thousand yen.*
> *I've spent all my money.*
> *I'm sorry to ask, but can you lend me some money?*

... we do accept credit cards ...
> *do* is used here for emphasis – don't overuse it. We would normally say:
> *We accept credit cards.*

British/American differences

British	American
the hold	the cargo compartment
overhead lockers	overhead bins
The bins haven't been emptied.	The wastebaskets haven't been emptied.
I've left my documents behind	I left my documents behind (American English usually uses the simple past tense.)
cancelled (p66)	canceled

Practice

1 Complete the sentences with words used in the dialogues and notes. Write the words in the grid to identify the European capital city in the shaded vertical row.

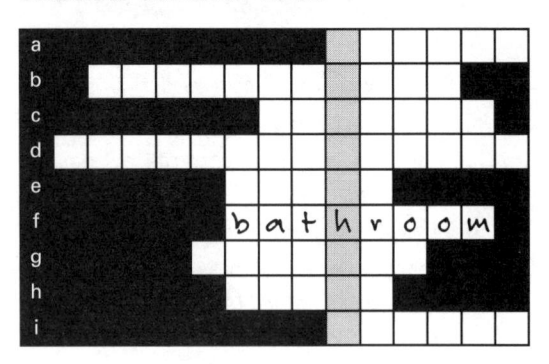

a Sorry, I wanted a return ticket, not a ....

b I have a .... in the name of Tiller.

c I'm keeping my fingers .... that I'll make my flight connection.

d We need to see some .... – a passport, a driving licence.

e If I'm very .... I'll catch the flight.

f I thought the room was en suite. I'd prefer not to share a ....

g I have a superb room with a south-facing *bathroom*.

h I asked for a window seat, not an .... seat.

i It took so long to clear passport control that I .... my flight.

2 Write what you would say in these situations. Refer to the dialogues and notes.

EXAMPLE: You are at the flight check-in desk. The check-in assistant insists that your hand luggage needs to go in the hold?

Is that necessary? It's very light/small etc.

a Tell the airline check-in clerk your seating preferences.

b Phone a hotel and book a double room.

c You arrive at your hotel. What do you say to the receptionist?

d Phone a colleague to say that your flight has been delayed.

e You have a tight flight connection. Explain your problem to the cabin attendant.

3 Complete the sentences with a preposition.

EXAMPLE: I don't have my passport ..on.. me.

a Please fill . . . . . . the registration form.

b Was the booking made . . . . . . the name of Kerry?

c Is there room for your bag . . . . . . your seat?

d The flight leaves . . . . . . half an hour.

e I'd like to hire a car . . . . . . a week.

f If we leave now, we should be there . . . . . . time.

g I asked for a room . . . . . . a bath.

h Unfortunately, I don't have any identification . . . . . . me.

4 Match the two parts of the sentences.

1 Someone will help you   a cash on me.
2 I don't have enough   b I won't make the connection.
3 I'll let you know if   c by 3 p.m.
4 I'm worried that   d with your luggage.
5 I won't be arriving   e a non-smoking room, please,
6 I'm hoping to be there   f I manage to catch the flight.
7 I'd like to pay   g until 3 p.m.
8 I would like   h by credit card.

5 Write alternative expressions. Refer to the dialogues and notes.

EXAMPLE: Is it necessary to reserve a seat?

Do I need to reserve a seat?

a Does the price include a seat reservation?

   . . . .

b I'll arrive at 11 p.m. or later.

   . . . .

c I'd rather pay in cash.

   . . . .

d A car will be waiting for you outside the terminal.

   . . . .

e I'll call you if I don't manage to catch the flight.

   . . . .

6 Rewrite these sentences in the passive.

EXAMPLES: No-one has made the bed.

The bed hasn't been made.

No-one told me about the fight delay.

I wasn't told about the flight delay.

a They put my luggage in the hold.

b No-one has cleaned the room today.

c Someone has already filled in the form.

d Someone booked the taxi last night.

e They cancelled my flight.

f They gave me a first class ticket.

7 Match the statements and questions with the responses.

1. Can I have your name, please?
2. I'd like to book a room for Tuesday night.
3. I hope you catch the flight.
4. I've missed my connection.
5. Can I pay by credit card?
6. The TV in my room doesn't work
7. What kind of identification do you need?
8. Where do I need to sign?

a A single or a double?
b When's the next flight?
c I'll send someone to look at it.
d Yes, of course.
e It's Ahmed Salem.
f Can I see your passport, please?
g Here, please.
h Thanks. Wish me luck!

8 Emailing

**Some useful phrases.
Listen to the recording and repeat.**

Hi, Jaana. Hope you're feeling better.
I'm afraid I won't be able to see you on Thursday.
Let me know when you're next going to be in town.
Look forward to hearing from you.
Speak to you later.

Your training manager has asked me to write to you.
It's about organising language training.
I'll call you at the end of the week.
If you have any queries, please call me.

Many thanks for helping out with the conference.
I would like to apologise for the problems we had.
Let's hope we have better luck next time.

I would like to invite you to lunch next week.
Are you free for lunch on Friday.
Let me know if you can come.
Many thanks for the invitation.
I'd love to come.

We are sorry to inform you that Raj Singh has left the company.
I was very sorry to hear about Raj.
Please pass on my best wishes.

Messages 1

A first contact

Dear Ms Hamza
Your training manager, Piotr Murawska, has asked me to write to you about organising professional language training for your company either in Poland and/or in the UK.
I will call you at the end of the week but, in the meantime, **if you have any queries, please call me** on 09809 or send me an email.
Yours sincerely
Esther White

A formal message

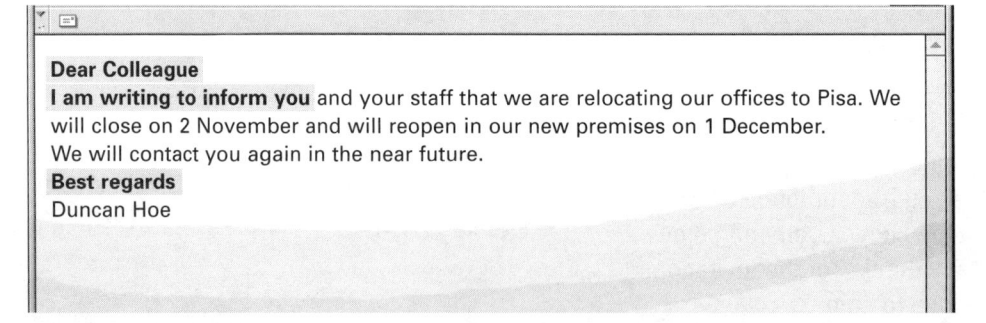

Dear Colleague
I am writing to inform you and your staff that we are relocating our offices to Pisa. We will close on 2 November and will reopen in our new premises on 1 December.
We will contact you again in the near future.
Best regards
Duncan Hoe

Everyday matters

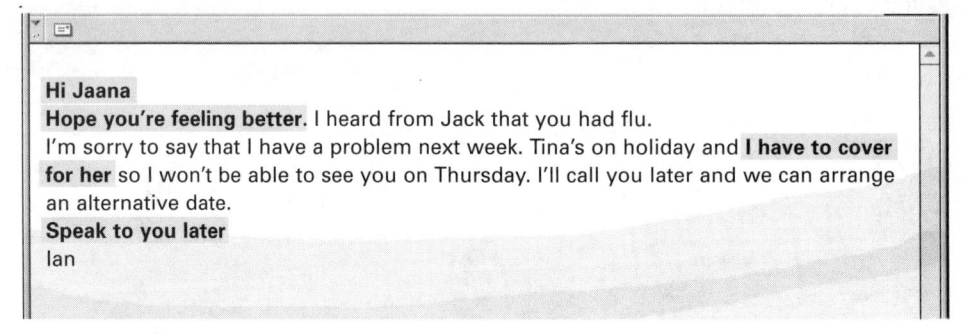

Hi Jaana
Hope you're feeling better. I heard from Jack that you had flu.
I'm sorry to say that I have a problem next week. Tina's on holiday and **I have to cover for her** so I won't be able to see you on Thursday. I'll call you later and we can arrange an alternative date.
Speak to you later
Ian

A future meeting

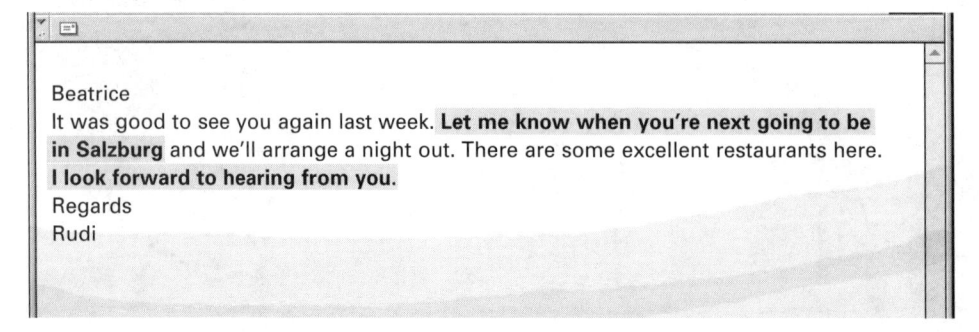

Beatrice
It was good to see you again last week. **Let me know when you're next going to be in Salzburg** and we'll arrange a night out. There are some excellent restaurants here.
I look forward to hearing from you.
Regards
Rudi

Notes

Dear Ms Hamza
> Use *Dear* with the person's title and surname when you have not written to the person before or when you have a formal relationship. If you are in doubt, it is better to be more, rather than less formal.

... if you have any queries, please call me ...
> This phrase is quite often used at the end of an email. Also:
> *If you have any questions, please call me.*

Yours sincerely
> In formal emails, we can use the formal letter-writing phrases:
> Start: *Dear Ms/Mr/Mrs Pringle*
> End: *Yours sincerely*
> Start: *Dear Sir/Madam*
> End: *Yours faithfully*

Dear colleague
> The use of a word like *colleague* is used when writing to an identifiable group in more formal correspondence. It can be singular or plural. Note also:
> *Dear friend(s), Dear member(s), Dear All, Dear Sir/Madam* (when you do not know the name of the person you are writing to)

I am writing to inform you ...
> Full verb forms (e.g. *I am writing*) are often used in formal communications. Note the less formal (and more common) alternatives:
> *I am writing (I'm writing) to inform you ...*
> *I am sure (I'm sure) that we can be of help ...*
> *I will call (I'll call) you at the end of the week.*
> *We will (We'll) contact you again.*

Best regards
> *(With) best regards* is a very common way to end an email and can be used in formal and informal contexts. There are many other ways to end, e.g.:
> *Regards, Best wishes, Yours, All the best*

Hi Jaana
> The common informal way to begin an email. You can also simply use a person's name at the beginning of a message
> (see **A future meeting** example on page 68).

Hope you're feeling better.
> Some other opening phrases:
> *Just to let you know that ...*
> *Sorry to hear about ...*
> *Thanks for the message.*

... I have to cover for her ...
> *to cover for* means to do someone's job while the person is away.
> *Who's covering for you?*
> *We're so short-staffed that there is no-one to cover for me.*

Speak to you later
> Phrases to indicate that you will be in contact later:
> *I'll send you a message later.*
> *Call me when you get this message.*

Let me know when you're next going to be in Salzburg ...
> A friendly note to end. Some alternatives:
> *You must visit us again soon.*
> *It was great to see you.*
> *See you again soon.*

I look forward to hearing from you.
> Note that we say:
> *I look forward to hearing from you.* Although quite formal, this phrase is very often used in emails. Also common:
> *I look forward to meeting/seeing you.*

British/American differences

British	American
If you have any queries ... (The term *queries* is not used as frequently in American English as it is in British English.	
Yours sincerely	*Sincerely*

Messages 2

Saying thank you (1)

Fred
Many thanks for helping with the conference. I'm very sorry that so few people came on Saturday – let's not organise the final session in the middle of **a public holiday** next year.
Anyway let's hope we have better luck in Yokohama.
Take care
Lucy

Saying thank you (2)

Dear Mr Reza
I am writing to thank you for your active participation in our conference. You really helped to make the event a great success.
I would like to apologise for the poor attendance at the Saturday afternoon session. When we planned the conference, we did not realise that **it clashed with the World Cup finals!**
Once again, many thanks and I look forward to seeing you in Yokohama next year.
Best regards
Lucy Lo Kit

An invitation

Hi John
I would like to invite you to be our guest at the Brazilian Grand Prix in March. The event is being held at Interlagos and **we would like you to join us for lunch** at the track and for an evening dinner in Sao Paulo. **Let me know if you can attend.**
Look forward to hearing from you.
Best regards
Pedro

Accepting an invitation

Dear Pedro
Thanks for the invitation. **I'd love to come** and I look forward to seeing you then.
Please send me details of the event when you have them.
Best regards
John

Declining an invitation

Dear Pedro
Many thanks for your kind invitation to attend the Grand Prix. **Unfortunately, I'll be abroad** on that day and I won't be able to make it. **I hope the event goes well for you** and I look forward to seeing you soon.
With best regards
John

Notes

Many thanks for helping ...
Friendly informal thanks. Note also:
Once again, many thanks.
Very many thanks!

... a public holiday ...
In the UK, public holidays are called *bank holidays*.

Anyway let's hope we have better luck in Yokohama.
Anyway is often used when we want to make a different point, to move away from what we have just said:
Anyway, I don't want to think about it anymore.
Anyway, that's all I wanted to say.

Take care
A phrase normally only used when talking to good friends. We do not use this phrase or others such as *Be good, Have fun!, Lucky you!* with our more formal business contacts!

I am writing to thank you for ...
Fairly formal language for saying thank you. Note also:
We really appreciate all your help.
We're very grateful for your help.

I would like to apologise ...
A formal way to apologise. A more informal phrase:
I'm very/really sorry about it.

... it clashed with the World Cup finals!
When two appointments in a diary *clash*, they happen at the same time.

... we would like you to join us for lunch ...
Note the other formal language used in this email. To be less formal, say:
Can you come to the Grand Prix?
I hope you can come to lunch.
Please come.

Let me know if you can attend.
A less formal way to say this is:
Let me know if you can make it.

I'd love to come ...
An informal enthusiastic response to an invitation. Some others:
That would be great.
That's a great idea.
I'll really look forward to it.

Please send me details of the event ...
An *event* is a special occasion.
It's going to be a very special event.
It took a long time to plan the event.

Many thanks for your kind invitation ...
Using a word such as *kind* emphasises the warmth of the thank you:
It was very kind of you to invite me.

Other ways of saying thank you:
Thank you for your excellent presentation.
Many thanks for the beautiful flowers.

Unfortunately, I'll be abroad ...
You can avoid saying *sorry* by using *unfortunately*:
Unfortunately, I'm going to miss the presentation.
I won't be there, unfortunately.

I hope the event goes well for you ...
A friendly remark when you cannot attend a meeting or event:
I hope it all goes well.
Good luck with everything.
I hope I'll be able to come next time.

British/American differences

British	American
realise	realize
bank holiday	legal/national/public holiday
apologise	apologize

Messages 3

Problems

Dear Serge
I have just heard from our French office that **they are having problems arranging the meeting** in Paris next week. There is a problem with accommodation as there is a large trade fair on at that time. All the hotels are full. **Do you have any suggestions?**
Best regards
Ian

Good news

Dear Eveline
Good news! We've got the RX contract! Thanks for all your hard work on this. **It would be good to get together sometime next week** to talk through some details. I'm free all day Tuesday and Wednesday afternoon.
Let me know a time that suits you and **I'll set up a meeting.**
Regards
Eresema

A general announcement

Dear Friends and Colleagues
This is to let you know that Will Pick is leaving the company on Wednesday 3 April. As many of you know, Wilfred has worked for us for more than twenty years. **I'm sure that you will want to join us in wishing Wilfred good luck** in his new job. We will be organising a reception for him in the canteen after work on his last day and we very much hope that you will be able to come.
Yours sincerely
Tara Gozo

For information

Dear Rosa
I am sorry to inform you that I will be off work for two weeks, as I have to go into hospital for a routine operation. I expect to be back in the office on 30 March. Helena Rallis will be covering for me while I am away, so please contact her if you need anything.
Best regards
Stavros

Passing on good wishes

Dear Helena
I was sorry to hear about Stavros. I am sure that he is keen to get back to work but tell him to take his time!
Please pass on my best wishes.
Regards
Rosa Fuente

Notes

... they are having problems arranging the meeting ...

Problems and difficulties:
We're having some difficulties.
There's a problem.
It's difficult to arrange.

Do you have any suggestions?

Looking for a solution:
Any ideas?
Do you have any ideas?
How can we sort it out?
How can we 'solve' the problem?

Good news!

Some enthusiastic responses to good news:
What good news!
That's great news!
That's fantastic/excellent news!

It would be good to get together sometime next week ...

To *get together* means to meet. (A *get-together* is an informal meeting, maybe a party). Other ways to suggest a meeting:
Let's meet next week.
Let's meet up in the near future.
We must arrange to meet up soon.

... I'll set up a meeting.

Another way of saying this:
I'll arrange/organise a meeting.

This is to let you know that ...

Use *This is* in formal messages to refer to the message you are sending:
This is to inform you that the package will be late.
This is to remind you to call Vera.

Informal alternatives:
Just to let you know that the package will be late.
I'm just writing to say that ...

I'm sure that you will want to join us in wishing Wilfred good luck ...

Note the use of *join* in formal messages.
I hope you can join us for dinner.
Please join us in the evening if you can.

I am sorry to inform you that ...

Less formal:
Sorry to tell you that ...
I'm writing to let you know that ...
I'm afraid I have some bad news.

... I will be off work for two weeks, ...

Some alternative expressions:
She'll be on sick leave.
She'll be away from work.
She'll be at home.

I was sorry to hear about Stavros.

Expressions of sympathy:
I was very sad to hear the news.
Everyone was very upset about it.
We'll miss him.

Please pass on my best wishes.

Some other sympathetic phrases:
I'll be thinking of him.
We hope he gets well soon.
Please pass our sincere condolences to his family. (when someone has died)

British/American differences

British	American
go into hospital	go into the hospital
How can we sort it out?	How can we figure it out?

Expressions of sympathy
There are not really any major differences between British and American English when expressing sympathy. In both, the level of formality used will depend on how well you know the people concerned.

Practice

1 Complete the sentences with a preposition.

EXAMPLE: She's ..on.. sick leave.

a   We will contact you again . . . . . . the near future.

b   I look forward . . . . . . hearing from you.

c   I'll call you . . . . . . the end of the week.

d   Please call me . . . . . . 456789.

e   Many thanks . . . . . . all your help.

f   Good luck . . . . . . everything.

g   I'm covering . . . . . . Raj while he is away.

h   He will be . . . . . . work for two weeks due to illness.

i   Please pass . . . . . . our best wishes to him.

j   We would like you to join us . . . . . . wishing Wu San a happy retirement.

2 Some of these phrases are used formally and some informally. Tick the correct column.

			formal	informal
a	1	Dear John		
	2	Hi John		
b	1	I am writing to inform you that …		
	2	I'm writing to let you know that …		
c	1	We're having a get-together.		
	2	We're arranging a meeting.		
d	1	I would like to apologise for		
	2	Sorry about …		
e	1	Let me know if you can make it.		
	2	Let me know if you can attend.		
f	1	I would be very pleased to come.		
	2	I'd love to come.		
g	1	This is to let you know about …		
	2	Just to let you know about …		

3 Write the sentences in this letter in the correct order.

　　　Dear Mr Green
a　Members of our sales team will present the service
b　After the presentation
c　We would like to invite you to the launch of
d　and there will be an opportunity to ask questions.
e　there will be dinner in the main restaurant.
f　our new courier service on 6 March
g　I very much hope that you can attend.
h　at the Grand Hotel at 6:30 p.m.
　　　Best regards
　　　Peter Pod

Dear Mr Green

Best regards

Peter Pod

4 Complete the sentences with the verbs in the box. Use each verb once only.

| inform | miss | know | must | hope |
| pass | join | call | get | thank | write |

EXAMPLE: I'm writing to . **inform** . . you that the conference has been cancelled.

a Your training manager has asked me to . . . . to you.
b I'll . . . . you at the end of the week.
c I . . . . you're feeling better.
d You . . . . visit us again soon.
e I'd like to . . . . you for all your hard work.
f Please . . . . us for lunch on 19 November.
g Can we . . . . together sometime next week?
h I'm sorry Peter has left. We'll all . . . . him.
i We were very sad to hear about Hubert. Please . . . . on our condolences.
j Just a short note to let you . . . . what's happening.

5 Match the two parts of the sentences.

1 I am sorry to inform you that I
2 I'll call you when I
3 Let me know when you are next
4 I'd like to thank you for
5 I look forward to
6 I hope that the party
7 Unfortunately, the event clashes with
8 It was very kind of you
9 I need to tell you what is

a hearing all your news.
b goes well.
c all your help.
d (going to be) in London.
e will be out of the office next week.
f to invite me.
g happening next week.
h get back to Cairo.
i an important meeting.

6 Rewrite the phrases and sentences in a less formal way.

EXAMPLE: Dear Tomas

Hi Tomas, Hello Tomas, Tomas..........................

a We will contact you in the near future.
   ....

b We would like to thank you for organising the conference.
   ....

c This is to inform you that we have changed the date of the meeting.
   ....

d Please let us know if you can attend.
   ....

e We trust that you will be able to join us for dinner.
   ....

f I will call you at the end of the week.
   ....

g We wish you every success in the future
   ....

h We are organising a party next week.
   ....

7 Complete the sentences. The first letters of the missing words spell a word you will 'appreciate'.

a It would be   **great**...   if you could come to the party!
b Please pass on my best   ....   to everyone.
c I would like to   ....   for the problems with the arrangements.
d Please   t.........   care!
e We are organising a special   ....   at the end of the year. You must come!
f I look   ....   to hearing from you.
g I can't come to the party, ...
h Let's hope we have better   l.........   next time.

Glossary

1 Telephoning

Dialogues 1

	Your language
I'd like to speak to Max Reed, please.	....
Hi Max. Simon here.	....
I wanted to run through some of the arrangements.	....
Sorry to keep you waiting.	....
Would you like to leave a message?	....
I'll get someone to call you when they get back.	....
I understand that she is looking after Sales.	....
Marco Stam is on parental leave.	....
I'm afraid she's not here at the moment.	....
Have we covered everything?	....
Anyway, thanks for calling.	....

Dialogues 2

This is Ann Forsell's voicemail.	....
It's about the meeting next month.	....
I can't make it.	....
Can you talk?	....
I'm in a meeting.	....
I was just ringing to check the time for next week's meeting.	....
Sorry, I can't hear you very well.	....
I'll just go outside.	....
If you are calling about an order, please press 1.	....

2 A company visit

Dialogues 1

Could you tell me how to get to your office from here?	....
After about two kilometres, you'll see a garage on your right.	....
Park in one of the visitors' spaces.	....
I'm calling from a service station.	....
Take the first left after the service station.	....

	Your language
Carry on for three kilometres.	....
I have an appointment with Hans Ekburg.	....
Do you know the building?	....
Mr Ekburg's office is the fifth on the right, along the corridor.	....
Hello, John. Good to see you again.	....
I'd like you to meet Lera Berman.	....
Did you have a good journey?	....

Dialogues 2

We're in the label business.	....
We employ just over 5 000 people worldwide.	....
It's growing all the time.	....
Tell me more about your mailing business.	....
We're a private limited company.	....
How long have you been on this site?	....
When was the company set up?	....
Let me show you around the office.	....
An open plan area.	....
I'll introduce you.	....

Dialogues 3

We're the second largest manufacturer in the country.	....
As well as supplying the car industry, we sell glass for buses and aircraft.	....
We run a so-called 'shopping search' website.	....
You can compare prices from various shops.	....
In my view it's far more secure.	....
In terms of sales by region.	....
North America accounts for 15 per cent.	....
The Chinese economy is booming.	....
We cannot compete with them on price.	....
We are well known in the market.	....
Transport costs make it very unprofitable.	....

3 Job information

Dialogues 1

Your language

I'm responsible for new product development.
I report directly to the CEO.
What does that involve?
It sounds challenging.
I hear you studied in Finland?
I did a degree in Engineering.
I was very interested in the job.
I usually cycle to work.
Are the hours flexible?
I like eating in the company canteen.
Excellent communication skills are essential.
Absolutely.
We should advertise with an on-line recruitment agency.

Dialogues 2

The atmosphere is very relaxed.
Everyone is on first name terms.
Don't you find it very hot there?
I have no regrets about moving.
$50 000 a year plus commission.
The cost of living in Kazakhstan.
The level of local salaries.
Neither have I.
The company really looks after its people.
I have free use of the company gym.
Promotion prospects are excellent.
How has the takeover affected the company?
About 300 people are going to lose their jobs.
Quite a few want to take early retirement.
There are no compulsory redundancies.

4 Presentations

Dialogues 1

Your language

It's good to see you all here. ....

I'd like to talk about our future plans. ....

First I'll describe our study programmes. ....

That's all I wanted to say. ....

That leads me to my next point. ....

So, next year's budget. ....

I'm afraid I can't say. ....

I didn't catch the question. ....

Could you bear with me? ....

Sorry, where was I? ....

You were just about to tell us some interesting news. ....

As I mentioned earlier, … ....

I'd like to finish by thanking you all. ....

You are very welcome to contact me. ....

Dialogues 2

Turnover rose in the year to April by 11 per cent. ....

Profits jumped by 20 per cent. ....

These results give a misleading picture. ....

A 'one-off' profit. ....

We're currently predicting a slow down. ....

Analysts are forecasting an upturn. ....

We're looking at a growth rate of between 1 and 3 per cent. ....

As you can see from the graph, sales have increased considerably. ....

Sales picked up in February. ....

Sales reached a peak in August. ....

The closure of our Lufwa plant in January accounts for the sharp fall. ....

Sales have continued to decline. ....

If you compare this six-month period, there has been very little change. ....

5 Meetings

Dialogues 1

English	Your language
I'm trying to arrange a meeting for next week.	....
Can you make Tuesday?	....
Is Juan coming by the way?	....
It should be finished by 3:15.	....
Just in case the meeting overruns.	....
He didn't want to miss the meeting.	....
I'd like to come over to Poznan next week.	....
Any day next week except Friday would suit me.	....
Could you check with Alex and get back to me?	....
I'll order some sandwiches.	....
Otherwise I'll see you in the office at 12:30.	....

Dialogues 2

English	Your language
Could you take the minutes, please?	....
I'd like to leave item four until the next meeting.	....
Can we look at item one?	....
What are your thoughts on this?	....
I was asked to find out what the people in my department thought.	....
The majority feeling was in favour.	....
Of the fifty people I asked, only five did not like the idea.	....
Does everyone agree?	....
Is that really necessary?	....
I suppose you're right.	....
The other point I want to make is this.	....
We must really avoid this in the future.	....
That's not true.	....

Dialogues 3

English	Your language
I'm just phoning to let you know.	....
Bad news I'm afraid.	....
What reasons did he give?	....
short-sighted	....
I thought I should let you know immediately.	....

	Your language
Anton has been having second thoughts.	....
He now thinks we've made a good case.	....
I'll call you tomorrow so we can discuss details.	....
Here are the main points.	....
Jaroslav to produce a questionnaire.	....
Juliet to research costs for proposed building project.	....
No decision made.	....
I've attached the draft minutes of the meeting.	....
Check if I've left anything out.	....

6 Entertaining and socialising

Dialogues 1

Would you like some coffee?	....
Do you take milk and sugar?	....
Can I have a soft drink?	....
Let me translate the menu for you.	....
Borsch – that's beetroot soup.	....
We're ready to order.	....
And for your main course?	....
I'd like fried chicken.	....
Medium rare.	....
Can we have the bill, please?	....
Excuse me, but could you tell me what this is for?	....
Do you take credit cards?	....
There's a cash machine just across the road.	....

Dialogues 2

Where do you live, Xavier?	....
Oh, I know Barcelona very well.	....
It's a great place for a holiday.	....
Did you see the football match last night?	....
So you like football, do you?	....
Where are you going for your summer holiday?	....
My son and daughter can go mountain biking.	....

	Your language
Do you have any children?	....
I don't know what to wear.	....
I'm sure they'd appreciate some flowers.	....
I'm sorry to hear that.	....
I can't really go into it now.	....
I understand.	....

7 Travel

Dialogues 1

Would you like an aisle or a window seat? ....
A seat in the exit row. ....
I'd like to book a hire car. ....
How would you like to pay? ....
A single to Munich, please. ....
Do I need to reserve a seat? ....
I'd like to book a twin room. ....
I won't be arriving until 11:00 p.m. ....
I have a reservation in the name of Perry. ....
Could you fill in this form, please? ....
We have a non-smoking room with a balcony
  on the 10th floor. ....

Dialogues 2

I just have this bag and a laptop. ....
The bag will have to go in the hold. ....
I'm not going to get to the meeting on time. ....
I've just missed my connection. ....
I'll let you know if I don't manage to catch the flight. ....
There will be a minibus waiting at the gate. ....
I'll keep my fingers crossed. ....
I asked for a non-smoking room. ....
The bed hasn't been made. ....
We need some identification. ....
I don't have enough cash. ....
We do accept credit cards. ....

8 Emailing

Messages 1

	Your language
Dear Ms Hamza	....
If you have any queries, please call me.	....
Yours sincerely	....
Dear Colleague	....
I am writing to inform you	....
Best regards	....
Hi Jaana	....
Hope you're feeling better.	....
I have to cover for her.	....
Speak to you later.	....
Let me know when you're next going to be in Salzburg.	....
I look forward to hearing from you.	....
Regards	....

Messages 2

Many thanks for helping.	....
A public holiday	....
Anyway let's hope we have better luck in Yokohama.	....
Take care	....
I am writing to thank you.	....
I would like to apologise.	....
It clashed with the World Cup finals!	....
We would like you to join us for lunch.	....
Let me know if you can attend.	....
I'd love to come.	....
Please send me details of the event.	....
Many thanks for your kind invitation.	....
Unfortunately, I'll be abroad.	....
I hope the event goes well for you.	....

Messages 3 | Your language

They are having problems arranging the meeting. ....

Do you have any suggestions? ....

Good news! ....

It would be good to get together sometime next week. ....

I'll set up a meeting. ....

This is to let you know that Will Pick is leaving the company. ....

I'm sure that you will want to join us in wishing Wilfred good luck in his new job. ....

I am sorry to inform you that I will be off work for two weeks. ....

I was sorry to hear about Stavros. ....

Please pass on my best wishes. ....

Answers

1 Telephoning

1. a leave b hear c hold d keep e call f want; press
   g get h say i hang; try

2. *Possible answers*
   a She's on maternity leave at the moment.
   b I'm afraid I'm in a meeting. Can I call you back?
   c Hello Peter, it's Fiona. Please call me back as soon as you can.
   d Please can you spell your name?
   e I'm sorry I didn't catch the number. Did you say fifteen or fifty?

3. a on b on c about d on e in f on g in h through

4. 1 d 2 h 3 b 4 g 5 i 6 e 7 a 8 c 9 f

5. a I'll tell him you called.
   b If I find the information, I'll let you know immediately.
   c If Peter doesn't come back from sick leave soon, we'll need to find a replacement.
   d If you push that button, you'll disconnect the caller.
   e What will you do if you don't find Sergei's number?
   f If I don't find his number, I'll call directory enquiries.

6. a handset b toll-free c This is d get e hang f turn off g area

7. h, a, b, f, k, g, i, j, e, d, c, l

8. 1 e 2 g 3 h 4 a 5 d 6 b 7 f 8 c

2 A company visit

1 a on b in c by d in e in f by g in h on i in

2 a registration b site c lift d corridor e profit f demand
       g partnership h reputation

3 1 e 2 a 3 b 4 h 5 c 6 g 7 d 8 f

4 *Possible answers*
   a At the roundabout take the second exit. Go through the town centre and then take the second turning on the left. The factory is at the end of the road.
   b Take the lift to the third floor. Turn right and go along the corridor. It's the fourth office on the right.
   c I've left my car in the space 'Reserved for Visitors'. Is that all right?
   d I've stopped just before a bridge, opposite a garage. I can see a signpost. It says that Fistularo is eight kilometres away.

5 *Possible questions*
   a How many people do you employ?
      How many people work for the company?
   b Are you a partnership?
   c How long have you been on this site?
      How long have you been here?
   d Do you like working here?
      Do you like the working atmosphere?
   e Where is your biggest market?
   f Who are your biggest/main competitors?
   g Can you tell me how to get to the factory?

6 *Possible answers*
   a I've left my car in a reserved space.
   b Could you tell me how to get to the main office?
   c I'd like to introduce you to our Marketing Manager.
   d Did you have a good journey?
   e When was the company set up?
   f We are among the largest manufacturers in the region.
   g We have an excellent reputation in the market.

3 Job information

1

a			f	r	e	e		
b			l	i	v	i	n	g
c		e	x	c	e	l	l	e	n	t
d		m	i	x				
e	r	e	t	i	r	e	m	e	n	t
f			j	o	b	s		
g	l	e	v	e	l			
h			m	e	d	i	c	a	l

2 a redundant b development c insurance d retire e stressful f owners
g leadership h promotion i challenging j responsibilities

3 1 e 2 a 3 i 4 b 5 f 6 g 7 d 8 j 9 c 10 h

4 a for b to c of d for e about f of g of

5

Crossword with: agency, takeaway, canteen, weekly, cost, allowance, graduate, takeover

6 1 h 2 f 3 a 4 b 5 e 6 c 7 g 8 d

7 a Neither did I. b So did I. c Neither am I. d So do I. e Neither do I.
f Neither was I. g So was I. h So am I.

4 Presentations

1 a by b up c with d between e by f in g down

2 *Possible answers*
   a Could you bear with me for a moment?
   b Are there any questions so far?
   c At this point on the graph you can see …
     This shows …
   d I'd like to finish by thanking you all for coming.

3 1 g 2 a 3 b 4 e 5 c 6 f 7 h 8 i 9 d

4 **Up:** a, b, d, g, h, i
   Down: c, f, j
   The same: e, k, l

5 a question b trend c point d picture e rate f fall/decline g point/level h period

6 a say b catch c repeat d bear e Take f gives g show h fall i account

7 1 b 2 c 3 a

5 Meetings

1 a make b cause c miss d happen e abandon f leave g report
   h give i cover

2 a **m**ajority
   b **i**tem
   c **n**ecessary
   d **u**ntil
   e **t**hrough
   f **e**xcept
   g **s**uit

3 a take b tell c make d set e made f having g rejected

4 a for b on c on d Of e to f on, on g in h in i at/through j out

5 *Possible answers*
   a I'd like to leave the next item until the next meeting.
   b Does everyone agree that the date of the next meeting should be changed?
   c Are you going to attend the next meeting?
   d I'm just phoning to tell you what happened in the meeting.
   e I've attached a copy of the agenda.
   f Just one more point.
   g What does everyone think about the idea?

6 1 f 2 c 3 e 4 a 5 h 6 b 7 i 8 d 9 g

7 a won't cause
 b 'll order
 c missed
 d 'll see
 e Does everyone agree
 f 'm calling
 g has read/read
 h to find out
 i attached/have attached
 j have had/have been having/had/'m having

6 Entertaining and socialising

1 *Possible answers*
 a Could you translate the menu for me, please?
 b Can I have the roast duck, please?
  I'll have the steak, please.
 c Can I have the bill, please?
 d Excuse me, what's this for?
 e Where do you live?
 f I live in Mijas. It's a small village in the south of Spain.
 g I'm planning to go to Bali for a week with my family.
 h I'm very sorry to hear that. We'll miss him/her.

2 a for b with c to d by e for f on g into h about

3 1 Can I *have*   the chicken and vegetable soup, please?
 2 Do you *accept* all   credit cards?
 3 Do you *know* if there is   a cash machine nearby?
 4 Do you *take*   sugar in your coffee?
 5 Would anyone like to *see*   the dessert menu?
 6 Did you *watch*   the basketball game yesterday?
 7 What clothes should I *wear* to the reception?
 8 What has *happened*   to David? Is he OK?

4 1 g 2 d 3 b 4 e 5 f 6 c 7 h 8 a

5 1 f 2 j 3 g 4 d 5 e 6 i 7 a 8 c 9 h 10 b

6 **play:** golf, tennis, badminton, volleyball, basketball, ping pong
 go: walking, climbing, cycling, snorkelling, diving, hiking, sailing

7 a nephew b aunt c cousin d uncle e niece

8 d, h, e, g, b, c, f, a, i, j, l, k

7 Travel

1

a						s	i	n	g	l	e
b	r	e	s	e	r	v	a	t	i	o	n
c						c	r	o	s	s	e	d
d	i	d	e	n	t	i	f	i	c	a	t	i	o	n
e						l	u	c	k	y
f						b	a	t	h	r	o	o	m
g					b	a	l	c	o	n	y
h						a	i	s	l	e
i							m	i	s	s	e	d

European capital city: Stockholm

2 *Possible answers*
a I'd like a window seat, please, in the exit row if possible.
b I'd like to reserve a double room for two nights, please.
c Good afternoon. I have a reservation in the name of (Badger).
d I'm just phoning to say my flight has been delayed.
e Excuse me, I have a connection to Dublin at 5:30. Will I have time to catch the flight?

3 a in b in c under d in e for f in g with h on/with

4 1 d 2 a 3 f 4 b 5 g 6 c 7 h 8 e

5 *Possible answers*
a Is the seat reservation included in the price?
b I'll be there about 11 p.m., perhaps later.
c I'd prefer to pay in cash.
d There will be a car waiting for you outside the terminal.
e I'll call you if I miss the flight.

6 a My luggage was put in the hold.
b The room hasn't been cleaned today.
c The form has already been filled in.
d The taxi was booked last night.
e My flight was cancelled.
f I was given a first class ticket.

7 1 e 2 a 3 h 4 b 5 d 6 c 7 f 8 g

8 Emailing

1 a in   b to   c at   d on   e for   f with   g for   h off   i on   j in

2 *The more formal phrases*
a 1   b 1   c 2   d 1   e 2   f 1   g 1

3 1 c   2 f   3 h   4 a   5 d   6 b   7 e   8 g

4 a write   b call   c hope   d must   e thank   f join   g get   h miss   i pass   j know

5 1 e   2 h   3 d   4 c   5 a   6 b   7 i   8 f   9 g

6 *Possible answers*
a We'll contact you soon.
b Thanks for organising the conference.
c Just to let you know that we've changed the date of the meeting.
d Please let us know if you can make it.
e We hope you can join us for dinner.
f I'll call you at the end of the week.
g Good luck!
h We're having a party/a get-together next week

7 a great   b regards   c apologise   d take   e event   f forward   g unfortunately   h luck

Key word: grateful